Praise for
All Politics Is Religious:
Speaking Faith to the Media, Policy Makers and Community

"[For] all of us who care, from a faith perspective, about politics as the instrument for peace with justice. [Approaches] religion for the purpose God intended, to foster understanding and faithful pursuit of truth, rather than as an excuse to disagree with and demonize one's adversaries."

—**Rev. Charles H. Straut, Jr., DMin**, Consultant in Ministry, New York Conference, United Methodist Church

"An acknowledgment of social reality and a clarion call for social action. Combines a rich religious perspective with practical suggestions for religious advocates who want to 'repair the world.'"

—**Rev. Dr. Richard Gilbert**, president, Interfaith Impact of New York State; social justice coordinator, St. Lawrence Unitarian Universalist District; author, *The Prophetic Imperative: Social Gospel in Theory and Practice* and *How Much Do We Deserve: An Inquiry in Distributive Justice*

"A distinctive, much-needed voice [in] the American debate on matters of politics and religion. Sharp insights, sanity and unfailing good humor."

—**Rev. Tom Davis**, author, *Sacred Work: Planned Parenthood and Its Clergy Alliances*; chaplain emeritus, Skidmore College

"This excellent, very readable book is a 'must have' for all people of faith, especially in this day of polarization…. It's like having your own personal media coach. I highly recommend it not only to spiritual and interfaith leaders, but to anyone involved in community activism who wants to make a difference."

—**Kay Lindahl**, co-founder, Women of Spirit and Faith; co-editor, *Women, Spirituality and Transformative Leadership: Where Grace Meets Power*

"With a wealth of personal stories from his experiences as a faith advocate, Rabbi Ross powerfully makes the case for an assertive, proactive yet civil faith advocacy (as opposed to a reactive one defined by the Religious Right) that is rooted in shared core values and effective messaging tactics."

—**Rabbi David Saperstein**, director, Religious Action Center of Reform Judaism

"Provides insightful communications advice for anyone looking to break through the usual media noise and spark social change on some of the most important issues of our generation."

—**Andrea Hagelgans**, vice president, strategic communications and media relations, Camino Public Relations

"With wit and passion, Rabbi Ross articulates his belief that all major political issues can be deconstructed to find a religious argument at their core. He then demonstrates how it is possible to move the political pendulum forward while encouraging civil discourse and steering clear of vilifying those whose views run in a diametrically opposite direction.... [This] guide book is for those who want to begin down the path of political activism without losing their religious conviction."

—**Michael Zimmerman**, executive director, The Clergy Letter Project

"Religious voices are a critical component in the movement for equality and justice. Rabbi Ross is extremely qualified to provide insight about how to effectively engage the voices of the spiritual community in the movement for positive social change."

—**Ross D. Levi**, executive director, Empire State Pride Agenda

"Clearly highlights the areas of social concern that often get lost in the barrage of words and rhetoric.... Give[s] new ways to talk about these controversial issues with civility and candor. A must-read for all persons of faith regardless of political perspective or religious ideology."

—**Rev. Vincent Lachina**, Northwest Chaplain, Planned Parenthood

"Offers tangible tools to amplify messages of compassion, unity and collaboration. [Provides] practical media strategies for restoring the integrity of moral agency, effectively raising our voices of inclusion and hope in the cultural conversation."

—**Kathe Schaaf**, co-founder, Women of Spirit and Faith; co-editor, *Women, Spirituality and Transformative Leadership: Where Grace Meets Power*

This Book Is for You If …

- You are a person of faith—clergy, lay leader, or faith community member—believing that the United States must do better at living up to moral values like providing for the needs of children and families, addressing immigration with fairness, and making sure that women can get essential health care, including contraception and abortion care.
- You are concerned about the many challenges to religious fundamentals, such as church-state separation and gay rights, and you want public policies supporting care of the environment and basic human needs.
- You accept that people will disagree on these issues and believe that we must discuss those differences with candor and respect.
- You want to become more comfortable and effective when:
  - Submitting a press release that promotes your congregation and faith
  - Writing a letter to the editor that makes your point with dignity
  - Preaching with conviction on controversial issues in a way that contributes to the harmony of the faith community
  - Submitting an op-ed that expresses your ideas and stirs your readers to act
  - Taking media interviews—for print, radio, and TV—with confidence
  - Building trusting relationships with elected and appointed officials

How to Use This Book

All Politics Is Religious is a resource for clergy and people of faith. The first half of the book talks *about* faith. The second half shows readers *how* to express it. Religious ideas in debates on issues like immigration, the needs of children and families, church-state separation, and reproductive rights, including abortion, are illustrated throughout the book. It speaks about spirituality, theology, and social values and is a research, writing, and preaching resource.

The second half of the book provides the "nuts and bolts." It presents new and tested ways to address the media, policy makers, community, and congregation. It describes steps to effective communication, including writing, interviewing, and preaching skills. It is a how-to to be kept handy for when you have a need— say, a press release to draft, a sermon on social issues to write, or a reporter's phone call to prepare for.

2/18/18

To Ann, with my best wishes,
Dee

All Politics
Is Religious

Speaking Faith to the Media, Policy Makers and Community

Rabbi Dennis S. Ross

Foreword by Rev. Barry W. Lynn

Walking Together, Finding the Way ®
SKYLIGHT PATHS®
PUBLISHING
Woodstock, Vermont

All Politics Is Religious:
Speaking Faith to the Media, Policy Makers and Community

2012 Quality Paperback Edition, First Printing
© 2012 by Dennis S. Ross
Foreword © 2012 by Barry W. Lynn

Library of Congress Cataloging-in-Publication Data
Ross, Dennis S. (Dennis Sidney), 1953–
  All politics is religious : speaking faith to the media, policy makers, and community / Dennis S. Ross.
    p. cm. — (Walking together, finding the way)
  Includes bibliographical references (p.   ).
  ISBN 978-1-59473-374-1 (pbk.)
  1. Religion and politics. I. Title.
  BL65.P7R67 2012
  201'.720973—dc23
                                    2012000832

10 9 8 7 6 5 4 3 2 1

Manufactured in the United States of America

Cover and Interior Design: Tim Holtz

SkyLight Paths is creating a place where people of different spiritual traditions come together for challenge and inspiration, a place where we can help each other understand the mystery that lies at the heart of our existence.

SkyLight Paths sees both believers and seekers as a community that increasingly transcends traditional boundaries of religion and denomination—people wanting to learn from each other, walking together, finding the way.

SkyLight Paths, "Walking Together, Finding the Way," and colophon are trademarks of LongHill Partners, Inc., registered in the U.S. Patent and Trademark Office.

Walking Together, Finding the Way®
Published by SkyLight Paths Publishing
A Division of LongHill Partners, Inc.
Sunset Farm Offices, Route 4, P.O. Box 237
Woodstock, VT 05091
Tel: (802) 457-4000 Fax: (802) 457-4004

www.skylightpaths.com

To my mother, Sara Mazon,
And to family members of blessed memory:
my father, Harry Ross,
my step-father, Meyer Mazon,
my grandparents, Nathan and Fanny Tuman, and Max
and Frieda Ross,
and my great-uncle and aunt, Harry and Mae Greenspan

Contents

Foreword

5/10/13

I have appreciated Rabbi Dennis Ross from the first time I met him at a big pro-choice event in Albany. Here was a man who had signed up for the long haul, decided to take that extraordinary risk and responsibility of caring about justice for all. He recognizes the duty of people of faith to be advocates in legislative halls as well as the responsibility of elected officials to be sure that their actions are firmly rooted in the commonly shared values of the Constitution, and not primarily in the scriptural understanding of anyone's holy writ or the words purportedly from "a higher power" now emanating from the lips of a powerful leader of any religious group. Rabbi Ross's view is that you marshal the facts, find the spiritual grounding, and then turn that into the constitutional imperative to allow people to make their own moral choices on the most intimate matters in their lives.

As we've learned from the run-up to many state and national elections, political leaders tend to conflate their religious and constitutional values. Politicians routinely claim fealty to the Constitution, but alas, it sometimes seems to be one from a planet other than Earth. On this netherworld, all things deemed constitutional also happen to fit perfectly into the candidate's religious worldview. This holds true not just for what Americans tend to view as hot button social issues—same-gender marriage, abortion, and prayer in public schools—but also issues that are less obviously religious. Ross is certainly justified in concluding in this work that "sometimes the politics don't look religious at all ... but sure enough, there's a religious theme at the core." The theme, though, is one too often rooted in what we Protestant Christians call "proof texting," an ability to cite a special passage from our biblical canon to justify anything we want to prove (often in the vain hope that no one else will be able to cite an alternative passage that might support a different, even opposing view).

Rabbi Ross is also a man who believes in passionate exposition of his views. He has never been willing to allow the anti-choice advocates or the fear mongers against marriage equality to prevail from the sheer power of noise or slogans shouted from the rooftops. Passion is not, of course, the equivalent of nastiness or ridicule but it is a stance that claims a moral stature to be matched against the rhetoric of those who would—for our own good, they say—tell us how to live our lives from the moment of conception until the moment of death as they define it—and pretty much every moment in between.

When I first came to Washington, I was a policy advocate (no one dared call us lobbyists) for the United Church of Christ. It happened that I was working on amnesty for Vietnam War resisters and Gerald Ford's fumbled "clemency program" was announced just weeks after I showed up. All of a sudden I had to do interviews with newspapers and even local television. It was all heady stuff for a person whose sole ministry to date had been serving a summer-only church in rural New Hampshire. I later learned that sometimes you start forming coalitions by grabbing colleagues by the collar (gently, of course) and convincing them this was "the most important new issue to work on." And then it helped if you could dream up a story on the topic to peddle to the evening news to confirm the significance of the matter.

What Ross has done in this volume is to walk us through the very practical day-to-day work of dealing with a now quite splintered media with new opportunities and new challenges. This requires being able to mix the facts with the feelings in appropriate measures for the audience you are trying to reach. Reading this book will not make you as glib as your favorite newscaster (who is probably reading a teleprompter) or as dashing or beautiful as a Hollywood celebrity, but it will make you less fearful, better trained, and more likely to be used as a source again.

Religion itself, as it speaks of ultimate matters of universal purpose and the source of authority, always needs to leaven its collaboration with governments and policy makers with recognition of the centrality of constitutionally-based communities and a respect for the autonomy of the diversity we find in a nation of two thousand religions and twenty million freethinkers, atheists, and humanists. Rabbi Ross, in this work, exemplifies this with rigor and eloquence.

—Rev. Barry W. Lynn, executive director,
Americans United for Separation of Church and State

Preface

5//4/3

Preaching to the Choir

2/18/19

I t happens to me all the time. I had just finished speaking at a forum in downstate New York. "We agree with you, Rabbi," I heard from the audience. "But you're preaching to the choir, spinning your wheels. Give your speech *upstate*. They need your voice up there."

Several months later, I found myself upstate facing a similar audience and a similar response. "We're with you, Rabbi," I heard. "But you're preaching to the choir, trying to convince the converted. You should speak *downstate*. Send this message to them." Here's my dilemma: If downstate says, "Go upstate!" and upstate says, "Go downstate!" where should I speak? In the middle? So this is what I said: "I'm glad you are with me. But we have to preach to the choir because this choir isn't being heard. This choir has to stand up and get really, really loud. This choir has to sing."

"Preaching to the choir," "spinning your wheels," "preaching to the converted": I understand the frustration of my audience. I know what it feels like to sit through that sermon, the one that tells me what I already believe. I might learn something, but once the sermon and service are over, I head home and nothing's different; the world stays the same. "Go preach to the *other choir*," I hear. "The one that needs to change. Go convince them—the people who want to ban stem cell research and deport immigrants. Go show them the errors of their ways."

My experience teaches that preaching to the *other choir* accomplishes even less. Most people are fixed in their opinions, no matter how good a speech I or anyone else delivers. It's as if our attitudes about social issues are hard-wired, set by instinct. So I went back to my own choir to preach. I talked about the pressing need for this choir to stand up and sing, and, thank God, more and more of us are coming forward each day. I wrote *All Politics Is Religious: Speaking Faith to the Media, Policy Makers and Community* to give voice to religious perspectives—supporting marriage equality, access to contraception, sex education, and abortion care, for instance—that all too often go unheard, if not unsung.

I have strong feelings about these issues, but you don't have to agree with me to get something out of this book. People of all backgrounds and persuasions have a lot to gain here. Of course I want the world to be a better place than it is, and we can start by using respectful, dignified, and honest dialogue that avoids personal attack and political ridicule. The moral and spiritual future of the nation is at stake. People of all faiths can find something valuable about religious communication in these pages.

I wrote *All Politics Is Religious* to my old self of almost a decade ago, back in the days when I sat with that quieter choir and barely raised a peep. Of course I followed the news and kept informed. I gave money to causes from time to time, and I signed a petition every now and then, but I rarely wrote a letter to an editor or called anyone in Congress—I didn't even know the names of my state representatives. I figured that having strong feelings and "all the facts" was enough; reasonable people would recognize that the other side was wrong, and someone else would surely speak up and set things straight. Then I started working as an advocate, and I realized how few people come forward. Like I did, many people expect someone else to speak out. But that "someone else" thinks the same thing, too, with the result that important viewpoints aren't being heard. Other communities own the forum—those opposed to the teaching of evolution in public schools or those who deny global warming, for instance. Their voices are very clear, forceful, and persuasive.

Meanwhile, when it comes to my positions, some folks are unaware that I, and religious people like me, exist. I wrote this book to help those quieter voices become better heard.

All Politics Is Religious has two parts. The first part of the book identifies and describes the religion in all our great national domestic policy debates. Sometimes the religion is obvious, as in a city council fight over allowing a holiday display in the public square. Sometimes the religion is just below the surface, as when evolution debunkers go to the public school committee to get "creation science" included in biology curricula. Scratch the surface of those arguments and the religion is right there. Sometimes the politics doesn't look religious at all—be it over the environment, the tax code, or national security, for instance—but, sure enough, there's a religious theme at the core. The second part of the book describes new and fresh ways to communicate. With a little help from *All Politics Is Religious,* a person of faith will be better able to enter the national conversation and speak with conviction and respect. You might think that religious leaders already know about communication and have little to learn. Preaching, speaking, and writing are such an important part of religious life, it makes perfect sense to assume that we already have these skills and have no need for building on them. The reality is we have plenty to learn.

Religious Communication: Between Two of Us and among Us All

Let's take a look back. *All Politics Is Religious* is the sequel to my last book, *God in Our Relationships: Spirituality between People from the Teachings of Martin Buber.* Martin Buber (1878–1965) set out to explain his Jewish faith to people of all beliefs and backgrounds, writing his classic *I and Thou* to describe God's presence at the heart of a special kind of human relationship he called *I-Thou.* Austrian-born Buber wrote in German for an intellectual audience, making *I and Thou* a challenging read for many. When Buber fled Nazi Germany to live in Jerusalem, he was asked if he would write in Hebrew. As the story goes, he jokingly responded that he didn't know the Hebrew language well enough to obscure his ideas in it! So *I and Thou*, for all the significance of its ideas, never got the full attention it deserved. I wrote *God in Our Relationships* to explain Buber's approach in a conversational voice, illustrated with stories and personal experiences.

At first glance, it may seem like the spirituality of his *I-Thou* relationship has little to do with political arguments and speaking with the press. After all, *I-Thou* means, as they say, *listening with all three ears*. *I-Thou* pays careful attention to the thoughts and needs of the next person. In contrast, rhetoric, lobbying, and addressing the media mean *barely listening with one ear*. It is all about selling an idea and getting one's point across, regardless of what the other person thinks. This is Buber's other relationship, the one he called *I-It*. This book picks up where *God in Our Relationships* leaves off.

I-It plays an important role. *I-It* happens when a customer is nothing more than a number to an account manager, when a student is nothing more than a grade to a teacher, or when an advocate sits down with a state senator and ignores an opposing argument to drive home a point. The *I-It* relationship can be cold, indifferent, tedious, soulless, even depressing. However, as Buber taught, the *I-It* is essential. Imagine life without the *I-It* of the surgeon's steady hand or the *I-It* of a bus driver's focus on the road under a sign that reads: "Please do not talk to the driver when in motion." We need the *I-It* in the businesslike and forceful conversation between the person making the news and the one covering it. We need the blunt lobbying visit that demonstrates sharp difference over a policy matter—and the political consequences that follow in the *I-It*.

I would never claim to know precisely what Buber—or any other historical figure—would do or say today about the way we live. Yet Buber had a strong commitment to the kind of social vision that this book embraces. Buber opposed capital punishment, even for a convicted Nazi war criminal like Adolf Eichmann. He called for cooperation between the Jews of Israel and their neighbors. He praised the Israeli kibbutz movement for envisioning and establishing a community based on equality. He affirmed the spiritual dimensions of intimate decision making, which is critical to the most contentious social and religious issues of our time, such as gay rights and access to contraception and abortion care. Buber took the same kind of leap from spirituality to policy that I am taking in turning from my earlier book to this one.

All Politics Is Religious is about speaking with dignity and respect. All too often these days, political conversations and disagreements lead to angry rhetoric and personal attack. This book would have *I-Thou* bubble over into *I-It*, so to speak. It asks that our political conversations are candid, free of invective, and marked by mutual respect. This book is my story, just like *God in Our Relationships* is my story. *God in Our Relationships* shows what I learned about spirituality in personal conversations. *All Politics Is Religious* shows what I learned about expressing religious values to the public, the media, and policy makers. Both books explore spirituality, religion, and communication.

The Most Important Lesson: Speaking with Emotion

In the wake of President George W. Bush's victory in 2000, a spirit of self-blame filled the conversations among many supporters of former Vice President Al Gore: We lost because we did poorly with our message. We were busy communicating the *facts* while others were communicating *feelings*. We were telling people what we thought they should *know* instead of stirring *emotions* that would lead them *to do*. We thought that having the truth was good enough. While we were *correct*, the others were *passionate*. And when people have to choose between passion and intellect, passion wins. There was a call for new language back then—words and images eventually put to use in Barack Obama's presidential campaign in 2008—but the nagging questions about communication returned and remain today. *All Politics Is Religious* provides new words and methods for expressing emotion and faith.

Working as an advocate helped me understand how language and ideas stir emotions that prompt action. People are more likely to respond with the heart than with the head. I looked back on my years on the pulpit and recognized truths that went right by me, that when it comes to preaching, for instance, people will remember *how they felt* when I spoke before remembering the details of *what I said.* Thanks to my media and advocacy training and work, I realized the importance of paying attention to the emotional, which made me a more effective preacher, writer, and teacher. It's not about how strongly *I* feel about an issue; it's about picking words that move emotions.

At first I felt uncomfortable stepping back from the intellect and reaching for the gut, but then I realized that's what the Hebrew Bible sometimes does. The passion of the prophets is a great example of emotional expression. So is the drama and suspense of Abraham's selfless and courageous negotiation with God on behalf of Sodom and Gomorrah, and Moses's success in convincing God to back down from imposing harsh punishment after the sin of the golden calf. Those stories stay with people; here we are, four thousand years later, still studying them and learning from them. Religious ideas and language circulated long before there were Democrats, Republicans, or any other party. Faith came first! The Hebrew Bible insisted on a social safety net of caring for the widow, the stranger, and the orphan, ages before anyone even thought of criticizing big government for being what it allegedly is. The Bible teaches a powerful and memorable moral message by reaching for emotions through engaging stories, poetry, and more. What worked then works today. This book has everything a choir needs to sing.

I wish I could promise that *All Politics Is Religious* will secure sound public policy—I can't do that. I wish I could promise that it will soften the tone of all the angry political rhetoric—I can't make that promise, either. But, at the very least, I pray that this book contributes a dignified and respectful religious perspective to the national policy conversations and empowers the faithful to make this world a better place for all.

Acknowledgments

This book tells the story of my work at Family Planning Advocates of New York State and its Education Fund, led by M. Tracey Brooks, president and CEO; Carol Blowers, vice president of governmental affairs; Dianne Patterson, vice-president of public relations; Ronnie Pawelko, general counsel; and Kathryn Alexander, Kimberly Bobb, Carolyn Ehrlich, Georgana Hanson, Debra Holland, Ruth Lyons, Dr. Grace Mose, and Valerie Trossbach. I thank them, as well as our former president and CEO, Joann M. Smith, and Karen Anderson, Susan Pedo, Alisa Costa, and Lois Uttley, along with Caren Spruch of Planned Parenthood Federation of America. Each one is a passionate, gifted, and determined advocate for health care for women, men, and families and I am very fortunate to have them as colleagues.

Several wonderful friends supported my growth into religious advocacy and writing. Rabbi Earl Grollman was generous with the lessons of his experience. Dr. Carol Ochs was a source of sound spiritual guidance. Rev. Tom Davis offered excellent insights about religion and gender. Marc Jaffe shared many great suggestions.

I appreciate the patient ear I receive at Congregation Beth Emeth, my synagogue in Albany, New York. I want to thank Rabbi Scott Shpeen, Cantor Glenn Groper, members, and staff for all they do, with special thanks to Benjamin Mendel.

The impact of SkyLight Paths Publishing and Jewish Lights Publishing, and publisher Stuart M. Matlins, is transforming contemporary religious life. I deeply appreciate the opportunity to work with him and his staff. I also thank the many people who carefully attended to so many details of this book: Emily Wichland, vice president of Editorial and Production, for making my writing clearer and stronger; Jennifer Rataj, Publicity manager; Barbara Heise, vice president of Marketing and Sales; Tim Holtz, director of Design and Production; Amy Wilson, senior vice president of Finance and Administration; and Daniella Cockwill, assistant editor.

The loving energy and encouragement of my wife, Rabbi Deborah Zecher, blesses all I do, and our children—Joshua, Adam, and Miriam—fill our home and hearts.

Introduction

How I Became an Advocate

After years of working as a congregational rabbi—visiting the sick, leading worship services, and going to plenty of meetings—I made a change. I became a religious advocate for reproductive rights, including sex education, access to contraception and abortion care, as well as stem cell research and gay rights. While I still enjoy part-time work at a congregation, this book is about religious advocacy and what I learned.

I thought that the professional change would be easy. After all, I figured that my new advocacy and media office—even one that jumps on breaking news—couldn't be more demanding than a synagogue, with all the pastoral emergencies, funerals, and internal politics. I couldn't imagine that a meeting with a state senator could be a bigger challenge than talking with someone about a life-or-death medical situation or sitting down with a bereft family to plan for a funeral. Who would think that speaking at a press conference would be harder than standing in front of a confirmation class and trying to interest a room full of tired but frisky teenagers who had already endured a full day of public school? Plus, I'd be working in Albany, New York, the capital of a progressive state. I expected to spend my time with like-minded clergy from many different faiths, something I have enjoyed doing throughout my congregational career. *This job will be a breeze,* I thought. But I was wrong. The difference was so great, I almost couldn't bridge it. I put my soul into it and learned a thing or two.

I learned that we don't have to agree on the issues in order to have a respectful conversation. Yes, I have strong feelings—a religious conviction—about things like immigration and health care, and I am a strong supporter of church-state separation. I am passionate about reproductive justice, including sex education for teens, making contraception available to those who believe they need it, and ensuring that a woman can get safe and affordable abortion care when she knows in her heart that she needs it. Religious people come to all kinds of conclusions about these issues—some I accept and some I don't. My work teaches me the importance of a respectful disagreement and avoiding the strident public rhetoric and personal attacks that threaten the moral fabric of our nation; we can have a dignified conversation, no matter where we stand.

I learned new skills. Though I was an experienced teacher, preacher, writer, and lecturer, I had to go through plenty of skill-building. Even with all the TV news I watched and the magazines and newspapers I read, I endured a gauntlet run of on-camera media trainings and mock interviews. I learned to "frame" my argument, to use a "message triangle," and to "stay on point." Though I was already a published author with two books to my credit, my writing underwent rigorous and painful edits and re-edits. I realized how writing for print (newspapers and blogs) is very different from writing a eulogy or putting something together for the pulpit or a congregational bulletin. I learned how to "drive home my message," all the while stirring up minimal discord in the faith community. It took a year—which felt like a dog year—but I mastered the basics and began earning the trust of a network of professionals in community organizing, government relations, and media within our office, across the state, and eventually nationwide.

I learned that media and government professionals really care what their stakeholders think. Like many, I used to assume that elected officials weren't interested in our opinions—and was I wrong! They read our mail and tally our e-mails. For instance, ten phone calls to a legislator can make a difference, especially on the state, county, or municipal level—particularly when it comes to clergy and voices of faith. It is the same with the media. People joke about the faithful not paying attention when clergy preach. How many stories are there about congregants in the pews falling asleep during sermons? Just don't tell any of those jokes to elected officials and reporters who pay close attention to clergy opinions. Our letters to the editor make it into print. Supportive policy makers become bolder when they hear from us: they speak up and call for a bill's passage.

Take an assembly member or a senator sponsoring a bill. He or she is committed to doing whatever possible to get the proposal through committee and down to the floor for a vote. They are thrilled when we come forward for them. They have a fight on their hands, even in a blue state like New York, and deeply appreciate clergy support. "I am glad to see you," they tell me. "We hear from the other side all the time. I can't tell you how much I appreciate your time. Now, please, please, please go visit my colleagues and ask them to move on this." Next thing you know, several wavering legislators have heard from so many advocates, constituents, community leaders, and clergy, they put their names on the bill as sponsors. A weakly committed senator decides to go out on a limb by calling around to ensure that house leadership moves the legislation forward. Legislators break from party pressure and vote according to conscience. Public opinion counts in the media and in state and national capitols—religious opinions in particular.

I was surprised by all the religious people in the halls of capitol houses and by the number of religious ideas in the debates. Religion is a constant, even in a blue state, where ministers in collars, nuns in habits, Orthodox rabbis, Muslims, and more come from all corners to lobby, just like pilgrims on a trek to a holy shrine to pray. They pray in the state houses too. After a rally of "Bible-believing pastors" denouncing marriage equality for same-gender couples, participants huddle in small circles to beg God to bring policy makers to see things their way. These religious advocates confront their opponents with lectures about their "sinful" ways or shower a gay elected official with prayers and demand that he "repent." They're not content upholding the faith in their own community; they want "buy in" from everyone at the capitol. They come in great numbers, demand laws that enforce their restrictive vision of God's teaching, and are a constant presence.

There's so much religion in government that I'll occasionally hear someone call for banishing us all: "We have separation of church and state in this country. Let the faithful stick to faith and let government run without religious interference." However, the reality is that religious people have the right—a responsibility, as I see it—to a public voice, just like everyone else. We live here and have a duty to contribute to the national conversation. We think, we vote, we pay taxes, we write letters, and we lobby—we are in the marrow. That's how democracy works. Plus there is nothing new about religious lobbying. Go back to ancient times when the Bible's prophets went about speaking their faith to power.

There's a critical difference between those lobbyists opposed to abortion, contraception, and stem cell research and me: *They want laws that impose their faith on others*, especially when it comes to restrictions on intimate matters like sexuality. Unlike them, *I want laws that protect against religious coercion*. As a matter of fairness and faith, I believe that people have the right to live their religious lives in private, without clergy or legislators barging in with restrictive, personal religious rules. After all, the American way means that our communities are neutral toward religion; our courts, city halls, and legislatures don't play religious favorites. We make personal decisions, living as spiritually as we determine, without government interference. Anyhow, religious people are never going away, not me and not those with opinions that differ from mine. So it's better to understand religion, accept that people of all religious backgrounds will be involved in democracy, and make sure that the government does not get into the business of playing religious favorites and regulating private life.

Finally, by becoming a religious advocate for reproductive rights, I got a new perspective on my faith. I developed an even deeper appreciation for the wisdom and foresight of my religious teachings, along with the teachings of a wide spectrum of faiths. I see now that they speak current conversations. This renewed appreciation of faith appears throughout *All Politics Is Religious.*

What's Inside This Book

The first part is a tool for recognizing the faith at the heart of national public policy conversations. It demonstrates how a debate may *appear* to be secular but is really religious. I explain the importance of seeing how faith, like a swirl of chocolate sauce in vanilla ice cream, runs through our policy conversations and gives them a particular flavor.

Religious people disagree over all kinds of things—God, the Hebrew Bible, and the afterlife, to name just a few. We disagree over marriage equality, contraception, and whether or not it is proper to use tax dollars to support conversionary religious programs. So when clergy come forward and say, "Hey, this is really a religious disagreement," we take the matter out of government hands and reclaim it as ours. We "reframe" the conversation as a religious one, properly placing it in the arena with all the other conversations where different faiths have different teachings. Our diverse voices demonstrate that this is an area that judges must not referee and policy makers must not tread. We are not asking anyone to change his or her religious beliefs. We are pointing to the American way, underscoring our insistence that the laws need to protect us as we live by faith and conscience in our homes and faith communities.

The reality is that our government is not capable of making religious decisions. Policy makers deal with schools, roads, hospitals, firefighters, and the like; religious matters are personal and private, beyond the scope of government's competence and responsibility. After all, when religious people wonder what happens to the soul after we die, the legislature doesn't pass a law to decide; you want your tax dollars being spent on that? When Christians consider whether Easter Sunday should be observed according to the calendar of the Greek Orthodox or on the day selected by others, the Supreme Court doesn't enter the conversation. Some religions forbid blood transfusions, the use of cars and electricity—is the legislature going to promote a bill to enforce those religious restrictions on us all? When rabbis disagree whether a piece of chicken is kosher or not, will the Department of Consumer Affairs play kitchen politics by comparing one rabbi's supervision with another's? When religious leaders disagree over the moral standing of contraception, abortion, and marriage for same-gender couples, it's not for elected leaders to step in and tell the people which faith has it right. Instead, they are to provide laws that protect us *all* as we arrive at our own determinations of faith and live by them. Decent people from the full spectrum of religious groups have a variety of opinions on our intimacy. Government officials aren't religious mediators; they have no business meddling in our private affairs. It is for us—people of faith—to discuss these moral values within our faith communities and for our faithful to reach personal conclusions that they live by. Religious disputes are properly raised and resolved within and between faith communities; it is not for the government to barge in, referee, and pick a favorite.

History shows that bad things happen when the state, merged with religion, establishes one faith perspective as the law; it's been awful when government has enforced religion. The nation best serves the collective interest by protecting private religious belief and expression, and this is where religious people come in: we "reframe" public policy disagreements as essentially religious and remove the conversation from politics, bringing it back to our homes and houses of worship, where it belongs. Of course religious organizations are responsible for following laws and policies that regulate a range of activities, including building construction, child protection, employee rights, and much more. But when it comes to religious matters—celebrations, personal practice, conducting a funeral, areas where reasonable people of faith can disagree—put up a sign: "Policy makers: Keep out!"

Part 1 of this book is about religion and the issues. Part 2 is a tool for expressing forceful and compelling arguments that are positive, civil, and respectful. Disagreements over the direction of the country and our communities need to be considered in the discussion, but personal verbal attacks and ranting about political parties don't get us anywhere. This book shows how to disagree without vilifying or ridiculing the opposition—as much as it seems the opposition may deserve it. This book presents basic media skills, something I never learned in seminary. As for my opposition and my voice, I know it's tempting to mock all those oddball biblical interpretations. And, I have to admit, I sometimes fall into that pattern (as I do from time to time in this book). Like you, like all people, I am also a work in progress. Nevertheless, it's time we reach for a higher level of conversation, as our faiths teach us to reach for. We have to at least try.

Ultimately, *All Politics Is Religious* seeks national change. The country and U.S. culture will be all the better for our involvement, but we need to learn new skills. We need to recognize that we—each of us as individuals—are responsible. We are the rightful stewards of our nation and can take charge of its direction. For sure, folks of other backgrounds think they own the place and are entitled to run it. Their efforts are meeting success, in the center of this country, with their eyes and reach expanding to coasts, east and west. So it's time we look at ourselves as the choir. It is time for us to stand up and belt it out.

Changing Negative Opinions about Organized Religions

I also hope this book changes negative opinions about organized religion. The public suffers through so much angry, strident clergy voices condemning people's private behavior, it's easy to assume all clergy think that way. I often hear, "Those religious people are all the same. They all want us to give up our way of life and start thinking and living like they do." I dislike getting lumped with all the angry others. All faithful, across the spectrum, are spokespersons for faith; we represent ourselves, each other, and all religious people. Observers judge us all by the bad conduct of a few. I wrote this book to say that there are other religious perspectives, communities, and ways of life.

People read about the tiny percentage of clergy who, in heinous abuse of their callings, have broken the law. To make things even worse, their superiors may have tried to cover it up. Beyond that, many people point to "religion" as the reason for international conflict and heartache and conclude that the world will be more peaceful without organized religion. No wonder many observers equate religion with condemning people, breaking rules, and starting fights. I want this book to dispel the negative perceptions, clear our reputation, and demonstrate how faith means trust, relationship, community, and love. I know that all of us in organized religion don't live by all that we preach. But we are not anywhere near as bad as we are sometimes made out to be—and our faith teachings have wonderful messages to convey. I wrote this book to reclaim the name of the people I have the pleasure of meeting and working with each day, to affirm the goodness of mutual aid and support that fills so many places of worship and religious communities. I hope that more people become open to seeing the positive role that organized faith plays. If you are not yet with us, I may tempt you to give a faith community a chance.

Finally, I hope this book helps religious people see that advocacy happens in many ways. Yes, there's lobbying and working with the media, but there's more. Let's say you are at a congregational dinner and there's a difficult member who is always starting arguments over politics and politicians. As members of the same faith community, you love him and he loves you; you have stood together through life's ups and downs, through many challenges and joys. But he carries on and on, with negative opinions about immigration, the poor, the economy, and more. You feel you must stifle your feelings at the cost of losing your appetite and ruining your meal. This book will not convert that congregant, but it will help you make a strong and respectful argument that preserves and may even strengthen your relationship. In turn, he may hold greater respect for your debating skills and your opinions and become less likely to pick a fight next time.

Entering a dignified conversation with our difficult friends and neighbors is a lot like talking with the media and policy makers. And the goal—educating people—is the same. So let's begin by looking at the issues.

3/29/16

Part I

How Religion and Policy Mix

1

Why We Hear So Much from One Side and So Little from the Other

Religion is at the heart of our great national debates. It presents a spectrum of faith perspectives on moral values, like providing for the needs of children and families, accepting immigration, and ensuring that women can get essential health care that includes contraception and abortion care. It also talks about the many challenges to religious fundamentals, like church-state separation and gay rights. And while my writing presents my strong feelings about these issues, I am also looking for respectful ways of discussing religious differences. I'll start with an example.

Give the reporter credit for trying, but she had no idea how to approach her assignment, covering a room full of clergy supporting abortion rights. She was a religion writer—for a national publication, no less, with a story and message typical of so many: religious people opposed to abortion set the agenda; religious people supporting abortion rights are the exception. All too often, people in the media and government just don't understand. They see us as a novelty, but we need to convince them that we are the rule, too. We do that by learning new skills and raising our voices. This takes a lot of work.

I am a rabbi in the Reform movement of Judaism, a denomination of more than a million members. I work with clergy from my and other Jewish groups, as well as ministers from houses of worship associated with Baptist, Disciples of Christ, Episcopal, Lutheran, Methodist, Presbyterian, Unitarian, and United Church of Christ denominations. I also work with Muslims, Buddhists, Quakers, and others. Our groups add up to the many millions. Granted, our congregations are diverse; not everyone in our communities has the same opinion. When it comes to issues like teaching evolution in public schools, gay rights, or abortion, for instance, we hear plenty from religious folks opposed and relatively little from the other side, to the point that it seems like even educated people, such as that reporter, don't take our supportive positions seriously.

It's tempting to blame the media by saying, "Reporters are biased" and "Editors ignore us." But that's not realistic or helpful. The media isn't a monolith; it's a diverse group of businesses, organizations, and people filled with many different opinions. While that reporter had no idea what to do with us, many media people do. Some even belong to our congregations, are well aware of us, and stand with us—and might bend *just a little* to make sure we get air time or are quoted in the newspaper. Others, who have never heard of us before or don't understand us at all, will respond to the fresh approaches that this book provides.

Another big problem can be seen in the numbers. Big as we are and generous as we may be, the math explains it. When it comes to people and money, we are outnumbered and outspent, outmuscled and outshouted. Recent surveys show that there are many more so-called religious "conservatives" than so-called religious "liberals"; the ratio is more than two to one. Plus, conservatives donate twice the money, per capita, than liberals.[1] Word of conservative generosity surprises so many liberals, with our "generous" positions on social issues like poverty, the environment, child welfare, and other topics. You'd think liberals would be more giving to houses of worship, advocacy groups, and the like, but the opposite is true; conservatives open the wallet and take out more. Faith communities that support things like prayer in public schools and religious displays in public places also encourage tithing—donating a tenth of one's income to charity. While only a small proportion of the faithful gives the full ten percent, and some tithe on after-tax income, not gross, they are still ahead when writing the check. All that talk about tithing encourages charity and, when combined with demographics, makes for better funding, organization, and visibility in the papers, on the Web, and on air.

Another point is about the message: clarity and force. When it comes to contraception, for instance, a simple "No! It's wrong! It's a sin!" makes for great press. Let's look at some specific examples: "Read my lips: no new taxes!" was the unambiguous and concise pledge from George H. W. Bush on accepting the 1988 Republican presidential nomination. People argue over what he really meant and whether he kept the promise. But there is no argument over the way those six stand-out words grabbed the media, an audience, and a place in American history.

In a more recent discussion of the economy, the Speaker of the House, Representative John Boehner, said, "This debt is also a moral threat to our country. In my opinion, it is immoral to rob our children and grandchildren's futures and leave them beholden to countries around the world that buy our debt."[2] That's a pretty clear argument: it's "immoral" to borrow for today on the back of tomorrow. But look closer, and it is much more complicated than a sound-bite. What about the moral obligation to children *now*? What will tomorrow be like when we compromise on education and child health care today? If today's kids fail, their children will fail, too! My faith says that all children are entitled; providing for kids, today and in the future, is the true "moral" obligation.

Speaker Boehner supported his position with a simple and definitive argument: "It is immoral." I am a making a more complicated argument: we have to strike a balance. He got media play. My argument doesn't. Even though we are considering issues of tax and budget—issues that seem secular—just as all politics is religious, the argument is really about religion. The Hebrew Bible struggles over financial policy issues, just like we do. On the one hand, the Bible demands caring for the poor, children, the old, and the sick; charity is the prime moral message. On the other hand, the Hebrew Bible also says that one's bounty is a sign of Divine blessing. A person could conclude that the Bible wants us to keep what we have and not give it away. This secondary theme is particularly evident in Genesis and the stories of the Matriarchs and Patriarchs. At the end of the day, though, the generous argument carries more sway than the stingy one. It is up to a religious person, like me and perhaps you, to look beyond the secular language and point out the argument over faith.

In a more obvious example, some religious folks are still trying to get religion into public school classrooms, particularly when it comes to attacking the teaching of evolution. Recent years have seen an innovative effort to dress up faith as science, using language like "creationism," "creation science," and "intelligent design" to sneak religious viewpoints into public schools. President George W. Bush reflected on his days as Texas governor saying, "I felt like both sides ought to be properly taught ... so people can understand what the debate is about." Responding to a follow-up, he offered, "I think that part of education is to expose people to different schools of thought."[3]

Sounds fair, teaching kids both sides. Exposing people to different schools of thought. Who could object to such a balanced and simple solution? But there is something very wrong when a public institution like a school balances science with religion. There is something very wrong with slipping religion into public education science class by debunking evolution and challenging something the overwhelming majority of science-based research endorses. I believe we should promote religion in the home and the faith community, not in the schools. My argument is more complicated and defies being boiled down to a simple "both sides" sound-bite; my beliefs are tougher to convey. And there's one real big problem: our folks are reluctant to speak.

When I was first ordained and I preached about so-called controversial topics, "There he goes again!" echoed throughout the congregation. "The rabbi is always talking about politics!" I'd hear from people who disagreed with me. This grousing was annoying to me and upsetting in the congregation, so I avoided talking about those issues. That's how clergy learn to keep silent. Once I became an advocate, however, I figured out better ways to preach without undermining the peace in the house of worship. It's easy to understand why many clergy prefer to play safe and raise only topics that don't cause rumblings. You don't have to be clergy to be tempted to shy away from these issues.

As the saying goes, "Never discuss religion or politics in polite company," as if a person breaks a rule by mentioning something controversial and starting a messy argument. When a neighbor spouts off about immigrants, it's easier to ignore the outburst and avoid kicking up more dust. When the morning paper reports a comment from a bigot, why bother with a letter to the editor when it's simple enough to just turn the page? When that angry senator makes the TV news yet again, it's not at all messy to grouse at the screen and act as if the problem will go away on its own. When a topic stirs strong feelings, it's easier to change the direction of the conversation, or to overlook it, and save one's opinions for the voting booth.

For a long time I kept quiet and made excuses: *Let somebody else come forward.* I told myself, *I live in a blue state and I don't have to do anything else. Nobody important is interested in what I think. I vote, and from time to time, I make donations. That's enough.* Thus, I joined the choir that barely mumbles and hums. All the while, those angry religious folks were singing louder and louder—and raising plenty of money—capturing the stage, swaying public opinion, and influencing laws in state capitols and in Congress, all as if I didn't even exist. We have to start talking about these issues, even in polite company. We have to go out and sing. The future of religious freedom and the destiny of our nation is at stake.

To those who say that religion belongs only in the house of worship or in the heart, see how the Hebrew Bible was the original publicist and the Bible's figures were religious lobbyists. Religious voices have always filled the public square, with the Hebrew Bible being the original "messaging" tool, "talking points" and "spin" included. If the Bible just said, "Cherish freedom," the lesson wouldn't stick. But the Bible got creative. It taught the community a captivating tale about plagues and miracles, of a powerful king brought down and drowned in the sea and the dramatic liberation of two million slaves. The Bible captured interest and drove home a lesson that stuck. If the Bible just said, "Workers have the right to a day off, no one is a slave to a job, and people have a right to be free," then readers would say, "Gee that's nice!" and go on their way. Wrap that lesson in a dramatic story—complete with a river turning into blood, frogs all over the place, a splitting sea, and a bush that burns unconsumed—and you've got an audience's attention. The story has endured for millennia, its values passionately transmitted from generation to generation. Look at that sound-bite—"Let my people go!"—coming from Moses in Pharaoh's court, spoken like a lobbyist armed with his playbook, taking on the most powerful ruler in the ancient Near East. The Hebrew Bible was the newspaper, op-ed, sports pages, and letter to the editor of its day.

Religious leaders invented the fields of media and governmental relations, and if we started them, there is no reason to stop. The Bible encourages us to take public stands and get the message out, to join the festivities or get left behind. We have a religious obligation to share our words, to preach the faith to all who would listen. Advocacy is a long-standing religious tradition, and there is a crying need for new and strong religious voices. Things have gotten so bad that people—even reporters and lawmakers—mistakenly assume that *all* religious people oppose reasonable things like sex education for teens, stem cell research, and marriage equality for lesbians and gays. Sometimes a legislator will tell me, "I didn't know that there's religious support for a woman's right to choose!" Quite frankly, I am disappointed when elected or appointed leaders don't know better. But we really can't place all the blame on them—some belongs to religious leaders ourselves; we need to be better at informing the public and people in power.

I look back on all those times I opened the morning paper to a pastor's railing in support of a crèche display in a public park or against gay rights and reassured myself with, "Oh, someone else will write the letter to the editor, so I don't have to." I now realize how many others were saying the same thing and not doing anything, all of us leaving the public in the dark and allowing our perspectives to get left behind. Meanwhile, angry religious people stepped into that vacuum to speak as if I and my opinions didn't even exist. If you are a member of the clergy or play a role in your faith community, I want *All Politics Is Religious* to help you speak with passion, dignity, and self-confidence, in a way that preserves peace in the worship community. We have a long way to go.

2

Core Faith Values

Protecting the Widow, the Stranger, and the Orphan

A n unusual and unexpected mix of Jewish, Christian, and Muslim leaders appeared at a Jerusalem press conference a number of years ago: Israel's two chief Orthodox rabbis, the patriarchs of Roman Catholic, Greek Orthodox, and Armenian churches, and three senior Muslim prayer leaders. These religious leaders typically avoid, if not condemn, each other; an occasional disagreement will lead to a fist fight. But that day was different as this diverse "choir" put aside their long-standing mutual dislike to sing of a common goal: halting a gay pride parade in Jerusalem.[1] Hatred and anger—especially over intimacy—take people who ordinarily dislike each other and bring them together.

Now, fast-forward across the ocean to New York State, to a similar scene as the state senate prepared to vote on marriage equality for same-gender couples. I had attended a rally a few days before the bill reached the floor. Opponents of the proposed law, who ordinarily go out of their way to ignore and avoid each other— all religious, by the way, not a secular person visible among them— stood together and raged against the legislation in one angry voice. The Jews among them shouted at me, "You're not Jewish!"

because of my stand in support of same-gender marriage equality. Representatives of a wide spectrum of religious and secular groups stood on my side, with me. When it comes to "moral values"—in Jerusalem and in Albany—Jews, Christians, and others, religious right and religious left, have more in common across religious lines than they do with some of their own.

Blaming the Victim: An Interfaith Activity

It happened again, in the immediate aftermath of Hurricane Katrina, as folks with diverse but extreme theological perspectives found something to agree on: the horrible storm was a punishment from God; the catastrophe was God's response to sin. Before we go on, I need to point out how many religious people heartily reject this kind of thinking. I, and many others, affirm the following:

- God's sheltering presence in the face of natural and social disaster.
- The potential for holiness in committed relationships.
- It is our God-given responsibility not to blame people for their heartache, but to help them out.

Before we talk about the things I affirm, let's look at some I don't.

Pastor John Hagee was founder and senior pastor of the San Antonio, Texas, Cornerstone Church and head of the John Hagee Ministries media empire. Pastor Hagee created something of a tempest when he said, "All hurricanes are acts of God because God controls the heavens. Hurricane Katrina was … the judgment of God against the city of New Orleans … because there was to be a homosexual parade there on the Monday that the Katrina came." And that wasn't just a gaffe; Pastor Hagee really believed what he said. When later asked to clarify if he believed that all catastrophic weather is the result of "the divine hand" and if there is "any natural disaster that is not a result of sin," the pastor responded, "If God is almighty and God is all powerful, God controls everything. If God does not control everything, he is not God. So the answer of that is yes."[2] According to this line of thinking—which I reject—there are no accidents. If something bad happens to you, you did something wrong and you deserve it. That's God's way.

After-the-fact weather forecasting is an interfaith activity—not in my denomination or in those like mine—but in others. Muslim cleric Yusuf Abu Sneina, the imam of Jerusalem's Al Aqsa Mosque, preached that Katrina's historic devastation was God's punishment for U.S. military presence in Afghanistan, Iraq, and elsewhere.[3] Rabbi Ovadiah Yosef, Israel's former chief Sephardic rabbi, alleged that Hurricane Katrina was "God's retribution" for the U.S. government's support of the withdrawal of Israeli troops from the Gaza territories, with a special eye of vengeance for the black people of New Orleans, whom the rabbi alleged lacked faith.[4]

Across religious lines that ordinarily divide, they all agreed that a sin brought the storm. However, they disagreed over the nature of the sin that made the wind spin—sex, U.S. military action, or something Israel did. They affirmed that nothing happens by chance and everything comes from God, in a theology of blaming the victim. Blaming the victim holds the suffering accountable for their misery. To some, victim blaming is an act of faith.

Back in the seventies, Boston College psychology professor William Ryan talked about blaming the victim in his book with the same name.[5] "Blaming the victim" means people bring hardship on themselves; it means suffering people are the cause of their own misery. And blaming the victim is all too common. Professor Ryan recalled an inner-city initiative to print and distribute posters reading, "Lead Paint Kills." The posters described the danger in eating lead paint chips and cautioned mothers against letting their young out of sight where they might eat the chips. On the surface, this looks like a wonderful effort, but look a little deeper. Truth is, parents aren't the *real* cause of lead poisoning. Rather, the neglectful enforcement of a city building code—failure to keep to the law and remove lead paint—was the *real* problem. But it's a lot cheaper and easier to run off a few thousand posters than to fix the paint. It's easier to blame the victim—in this case, the parent who is expected to be the child's 24/7 cop.

Professor Ryan points out that victim blaming has a caring ring to it, a misdirected compassion and patronizing attitude that says, "You poor thing. If only you were a little smarter, a little better, more responsible, your kid would not get sick." Blaming the victim lets the blamer have it both ways, so to speak. It gives a pretense of offering advice—"Lead paint kills! Don't leave your kid alone!" And it lets the blamer off the hook, spared of having to do much of anything else to make things better: "I put up posters! What more do you want from me?" Of course it makes sense to inform parents of the dangers of lead paint. But if a poster is all that happens, landlords and the city government get off easy, and innocent kids get sick. We blame the victim when we say parents, who wish they had jobs that paid enough to afford decent housing, are responsible for the lead poisoning of their children.

The Hebrew Bible offers a classic example of victim blaming in the book of Job. Job, a righteous soul, suddenly loses his house, livestock, children, and then his health. Job's three best friends arrive to offer sympathy at first, then they blame Job for bringing on his misery himself. They tell Job that he wasn't righteous at all; he was a sinner paying the price for his misdeeds. After all, in their minds everything comes from God, so if you are suffering, you must have sinned. But as the book ends, God supports Job. God speaks out of a whirlwind, claiming that human hardship is just one of those things that no mortal will be able to understand or explain. There *are* victims in life, victims that deserve no blame.

There is plenty at stake in victim blaming. Blaming lets Job's friends get away with holding on to their firm conviction in the shaky belief that the world is a fair place and that people get what they deserve. It lets them spout off about how good is always rewarded and bad always punished. Blaming Job preserves their unrealistic worldview. All this blaming gives an impression that the friends are offering real help, all the while doing nothing more than running their mouths. Job is a victim, all right, but he bears no blame.

We see the roots of victim blaming in legends of rags to riches stories. It starts with the erroneous assumption that each person is the maker of his or her destiny, that anything is possible, that if you work hard, you will conquer the world all on your own, without anyone's help. If you want to be rich, then "a penny saved is a penny earned" and "the early bird gets the worm." If you want to be healthy, then "early to bed early to rise" and "just give up smoking and lose weight." On the flip side of these worn sayings is an often unspoken assumption: If you fail, you must have messed up. If you get sick, you never had the discipline to put down the cigarette or the fork. If you are out of work, well, you didn't exert yourself. Never mind that your inner-city school never gave you a proper education. Never mind that your health is bad because your parents couldn't afford to bring you to a doctor, let alone take time from work to do it. In a world where we blame the victim, *you* failed and it's *your* fault. Yet my faith perspective wants me to move from victim blaming to prevention.

Isn't it better to protect people to begin with? We could probably reduce the impact of car accident injuries with more ambulances and more training for medical workers. But wouldn't it be better to prevent these accidents in the first place by fixing potholes, ensuring cars have working brakes, and making sure people don't drink and drive? Instead of responding to tooth decay by drilling and filling cavities and blaming kids for eating too many sweets, we fluoridate water to reduce the number of cavities in the first place. Isn't it better to preempt damage instead of just repairing it? We turn away from victim blaming by admitting that some people don't have equal opportunity to get child care, good work, good schools, good homes, and health care. Beyond that, we can promote policies that protect victims, the injured, the weak, and the powerless. I know that we sometimes add to our pain. But it is not for us to apportion blame—better to prevent pain in the first place and ease suffering when there is misfortune.

Affirming Positive Religious Values

So far, I have explored things that *I don't do. I don't* blame God for natural disasters like hurricanes, tornados, and earthquakes;

these catastrophes happen on their own. *I don't* use the Bible or the pulpit to bully people with threats of Divine punishment. *I don't* misuse theology to smack down people who are already down. And I *don't* blame people for their misfortune. These are things that *I don't believe or do.* It's time to consider *what I affirm.* Our choir spends plenty of time grumbling about what others do wrong; let's sing about making the world right. We begin by identifying positive religious values, such as the following:

- Caring for the powerless
- Softening harsh justice with compassion
- Affirming a positive vision of the end of days
- Upholding moral agency as a religious value
- Strengthening church-state separation

Caring for the Powerless

The issue of immigration has stirred strong feelings from the very beginning. Even the most casual student of Jewish-American history knows that in 1654, Peter Stuyvesant, colonial governor of New Amsterdam (today's Manhattan), tried to expel all twenty-three of the first Jewish immigrants to America, Brazilian refugees with no place else to go. Never mind that Stuyvesant and his supporters were new Americans themselves. From then till now, hostility toward immigrants and the surrounding rhetoric have waxed and waned, depending on the mood of the day.

When I think of immigration, I am reminded of my own family origins. My great-grandfather came to the United States from Russia in 1885. As promising a year as it was for him, it was difficult for many other immigrants, especially those from China, who suffered from violence, threats, discrimination, and harassment across the country. Outside Seattle, Washington, for instance, Chinese immigrants were given an ultimatum: leave within twenty-four hours or be shot to death. In Cheyenne, Wyoming, immigrants were ordered to flee or face being tarred, feathered, and driven from the city.[6] Following violence in Augusta, Georgia, authorities received a petition to prevent additional Chinese settlement. San

Francisco heard calls for boycotting businesses employing Chinese, with allegations they were taking jobs from others, even though no one else around was willing to do the kind of work the Chinese immigrants did; different times—same argument. Today, when it comes to immigration, very little has changed.

Immigration is a religious issue—for my people, my family, and for us all. In the days of the Hebrew Bible, when a stranger—a particular class of foreigner—was unwelcome or excluded from so many countries, the Hebrew Bible extended a measure of protection as part of what grew to become a biblical social safety net. We read, "When a stranger lives in your land, you shall not wrong that stranger. The stranger living with you shall be like one of your citizens. You shall love the stranger as yourself, because you were strangers in the land of Egypt. I am your Eternal God" (Leviticus 19:33–34).[7] Three dozen times, more than any other commandment, the Hebrew Bible calls upon us to provide—and never to exploit.

The Bible gets this idea from the slave experience in Egypt—Israel's 430 years in bondage under the Pharaohs. The early leaders of the people of Israel (the biblical Jacob and his extended family) fled their homeland in Canaan during a time of drought and famine, seeking food in the fertile Egyptian Nile region. The Egyptians initially welcomed this nomad family, but as time passed, they enslaved them. The Hebrew Bible recalled this slave history and invoked God's example: as God liberated them from the heartache of bondage, so we are to help other oppressed souls to freedom—from slavery, oppression, hunger, homelessness, and fear. The Bible considered the redemption from slavery and taught the responsibility to spare others the agony we knew, and to care and provide for them.

The Hebrew Bible went on to extend the protections of the stranger to others—the widow and the orphan—safeguarding an entire social category from exploitation by the more privileged and powerful. In an additional measure of care for the powerless underclass, the Bible forbade placing a stumbling block before the blind. Later, the Rabbis took the concept further by outlawing exploitation of those unaware or unseeing of the hazards of life—be they physical, economic, social, or otherwise. Insistence on honest weights and measures prevented a merchant from gouging an unknowing customer. The hungry and poor sustained themselves by gleaning the corners of the fields for produce, which no one else, not even the field owner, could take. The Bible demanded that a day laborer be paid at sunset; delayed wages equaled theft. All these protections combined to demonstrate the social safety net that was the centerpiece of biblical teaching: protect and care for the vulnerable, starting with the stranger. Today, the trio of widow, stranger, and orphan stands in a broader context: the widow symbolizes the woman and her need for an extra measure of attention when it comes to her health care; the stranger is the immigrant; and the orphan is the youth, where I focus next.

Softening Harsh Justice with Compassion: The Orphan and Youth

The Vietnam War era from the late 1960s through 1975 placed the nation's young at the center of the great debate. When leaders from President Richard Nixon to presidential contender Alabama governor George Wallace called for "law and order," they weren't talking about the TV series; it didn't exist yet. "Law and order" meant cracking down on youth and others—everyone from "draft dodgers" to "welfare cheats"—allegedly disrespectful of government and authority.

It was a frightening time. Riots protesting war abroad and poverty at home swept across big cities and college campuses. Many social critics pointed to "permissiveness" as an underlying cause: overindulgent parents bred and raised a generation of self-centered children who grew to threaten the national integrity. Critics pointed to "permissiveness" as the root cause of a range of social ills, from student violence to draft dodging and urban mayhem. The mantra of "sex, drugs, and rock and roll" added to the distress over the way many youth appeared to some critics: dirty, in shabby dress, and long-haired. Their behavior got slammed as unruly, irresponsible, defiant, and disrespectful of elders and authority alike. The work ethic, it seemed, was dying or dead. So politicians called for "law and order" to set things straight.

In one notable extreme example of behavior and rhetoric, protestors blocked President Lyndon Johnson's motorcade. If that wasn't bad enough, Governor Wallace referred to them as "anarchists" and promised that if protestors did that to him, "It'll be the last automobile they'll want to lie down in front of."[8] Forget about due process. Forget about proper grammar, too. There would be "law and order"—swift, severe, and summary justice—to resolve the nation's problems of the day. As a rabbi looking back on those painful times and the surrounding rhetoric, I believe that anyone breaking the law must be held accountable and punished. All politics was religious then, too.

Let's turn to the Hebrew Bible, which teaches:

> When a parent has a stubborn and rebellious son, who does not obey his father or mother even after they discipline him, his father and mother shall take hold of him and bring him to the elders of his town holding court at the city gate. They shall say to the elders of his town, "This son of ours *is* stubborn and rebellious. He does not obey us. He is a glutton and a drunkard." Then the residents of his town shall stone him to death. This is how you will sweep evil from your midst, and all Israel will hear and be afraid.
>
> (Deuteronomy 21:18–21)

There's quick justice and cold-blooded deterrence: firm, swift, clean, and complete. It punishes misdeeds and keeps society pure. Running a youth over with a car, stoning—no difference. Hold people responsible and set an example for others.

Needless to say, Jews don't do this today. When it came up for debate by the rabbis in the centuries that followed, no rabbi could point to any such sentencing in all of Jewish history, except for one who recalled a single incident. The vast majority of the rabbis were very uncomfortable with capital punishment for this and other crimes. They were teachers and parents who understood the challenges of growing up and raising kids. Their real-world experience gave them a sensitive understanding of human nature. As parents of teens themselves, they knew what it was like to try to teach moral behavior to the young—and what it was like to fail. They loved the Bible and didn't want to directly challenge its teachings, so instead, they made it almost impossible to reach a capital conviction.

The Rabbis of later Jewish legal books, the Mishnah and the Talmud, went out of their way to lower the chances of serious punishment. Noting the Hebrew stipulates a *ben*, not *bat* (a *son*, not a *daughter*), the Rabbis excluded half the population from prosecution under the law, even though a young woman can be equally defiant. Then they noted that the Hebrew Bible maintains that both father *and* mother must present the claim; one parent cannot bring forward a child without the support of the other, case closed. The parents must be legally married to each other, and either one can withdraw a complaint prior to conviction and the youth would be spared. Then the Rabbis noted that the Hebrew word *ben*, or "son," is not *yeled* or *bar*. They insisted that *ben* points to a tiny time window of no more than six months around bar mitzvah age, preventing conviction of anyone younger or older. The Rabbis defined gluttony and drunkenness as the consumption of large quantities of stolen meat and wine in the company of no-gooders; no less and no different an offense would do. The meat must be kosher; pork would not qualify. As with any capital crime, the Rabbis insisted that the young man be warned of the specific law in advance, and there must be two witnesses to the sin. They said only the second conviction warrants death—the first just gets a flogging and a warning.

So the Rabbis did their best to prevent conviction of the *ben sorer* (stubborn and rebellious son). They had a deep and abiding respect for the law, and at the same time, an aversion to cold-blooded justice, especially when it came to youth. They refused to leave any child behind. In the same vein, the Rabbis were reluctant to foist the full scope of punishment on anyone. Time and time again, the

Rabbis blended justice with mercy, often holding people accountable for their actions and moderating the severest sentence. Not that they let a criminal off the hook; they believed in justice, but mixed with mercy. After all, the Hebrew Bible has God say, "It is not the death of the sinners I seek, but that they turn from their evil ways and live" (Ezekiel 33:11).

Echoing that theme, the Rabbis tell the following story in the Talmud: Some youths in Rabbi Meir's neighborhood were aggravating him, and out of upset, he prayed for their deaths. His wife, Bruriah, asked him, "How can you think such a prayer is allowed? Pray for an end to sin, and sin having ended, there will be no more evil. Pray for them to stop and repent." So the rabbi prayed for them and they repented.[9] Rabbi Meir followed his wife's good advice; problem addressed. You don't pray for bad things to happen to other people, even if they deserve it. God doesn't answer or want those prayers. You pray for improvement. So he didn't bring the kids in for flogging or stoning, and he didn't ask their parents to do that either. He asked God to help them. He tempered justice with mercy.

In another legend: A parable is told of a monarch who owned delicate glass cups. Said the monarch, "If I pour hot water into them, they will burst. Cold water will make them shatter." The monarch mixed hot and cold water and poured it into the glass cups, and so they stood. In the same way, God said, "If I create the world by the rule of mercy alone, the sins will be many. With the rule of justice alone, it would not stand. So I will create it with both justice and mercy, so it will endure."[10] Not all justice, not all mercy. A balance of the two is the goal.

My End Times Vision

Religious literature and leaders spend plenty of time thinking about and addressing the final times. Some faiths affirm judgment in the hereafter. Some speak of an end of days when God hands out whatever we deserve. And some propose that the righteous will be suddenly taken by God in "rapture," leaving behind their worldly goods—homes, money, and clothing—along with the stunned rest of us to be confronted by unprecedented world conflict and hardship. There is a range of beliefs.

I have trouble with the dire prophecies of God's judgment and punishment. No one is really sure what God has in store for us. Only God knows. Even as I believe God is unknowable, my faith says that God fills with love. I affirm a loving, forgiving God, who is very much a mystery that no human mind can comprehend. When we consider end times, my faith, as I suspect yours, has a vision. My vision starts with the book of Genesis of the Hebrew Bible, with God's six days of creation followed by the holy Sabbath, when God stops work. The Bible teaches to do as God—to cease work at the close of the six-day week, we and our entire households. Even our beasts of burden partake of God's day of holiness and blessing. As the Hebrew Bible progresses, we recall the Exodus from Egypt, the flight from bondage, and the promise of freedom. Work and cessation from work come to everyone, one day of each week, each week of the year. Utopia begins with the Sabbath.

Next, the Bible moves from one day in seven to one year in seven, and the sabbatical year. The land lies fallow during the sabbatical year; planting and harvest cease as the people eat of the stored bounty of years prior. The hungry and the poor, the widow, the stranger, and the orphan feed themselves with what grows in the field on its own. The beasts roam and eat in peace. Debts are cancelled and indentured servants go free. Then the Bible counts seven sets of seven years, for a total of forty-nine. In the fiftieth year, the sound the shofar, the ram's horn, announces a year of jubilee when all land returns to its original owners and indentured servants return to their homelands. No one is left behind.

Seven days, seven years, and seven sets of seven years all add up to the perfect society; the rich and the poor stand the same in the eyes of God, and the land and nature are restored. Real estate gets returned; the economic disparities and the power they bring are reduced. What you once owned comes back, all in a social, economic, political, ecological harmony—the ultimate theological reordering. Like God, we are spared the worry and effort of labor.

When we live the life of the Sabbath, every human being and living being is equal and free.

It's a dream, of course. While there was a Sabbath in the time of the Bible, no one knows for sure that the cycles of the years came to be. Maybe it was just a far-fetched, idealistic dream, but it is my utopian vision. There's a balance of justice and mercy at the heart my faith. At the end of the day, there is God's love and the promise of equality and freedom. Of course, I am upset when people do wrong, and I believe that those who break the rules must be held accountable. However, we step back from imposing the full force of punishment and anticipate an end time with hope, a day when suffering and evil cease. Looking around today, many leaders echo that old "law and order" theme, as policy makers present themselves as tough on crime, national security, immigration, and terrorism. But even as we need security, we need to avoid using threats of punishment to advance a religious and political end; it's wrong to use faith as a club over the head.

What's your utopian vision? Are all ultimately equal? Or does your vision reward the handful of faithful and punish those who stray from religious strictures? Does it embrace rigid rules imposed by an angry God? Or does it teach us to be tolerant of mortal short-comings? Will your vision recognize what it means to be human, open to diversity of opinion, moderate in anger, learning and grow-ing in truth? Will it see pollution banished and reversed, human health protected, and life extended? Will it give all children a sound education, comprehensive health care, safe and secure homes that are free of violence and filled with support, love, and direction? There is more to my God than punishment. My God fills with love. Yes, the Hebrew Bible would have us stop blaming the victim and instead protect and care for the woman, the immigrant, and the youth—the widow, the stranger, and the orphan. But before we turn to the ways we communicate these essential concepts in the public square, there are two more values to consider: moral agency and church-state separation.

3

Core Faith Values
Moral Agency

2/24/18

On a typical day, lobbyists, reporters, government staff, assembly members, and senators flow through the stone-walled corridors of the New York State capitol building as smoothly as water down the nearby Hudson River. But this day was different, with a marriage equality vote heading downstream at us.

I reached the capitol and halls overstuffed with agitated people and their posters, hymns, and chants—"God says 'No!'" from one side and "God says 'Yes!'" from the other—a religious shouting match under the glare of TV news lights. A group of opponents saw my *kipah* and called, "Rabbi, you belong with us!" To their upset, I snaked through the throngs to join supporters, turning myself into a recipient of their jeers. An opponent stood a few feet in front of me, pointed to his Bible, and insisted I should know better. Yelled one, "You call yourself a rabbi? Didn't you read the book of Leviticus?" Responded another, "What do you expect? The Bible calls Jews a 'stiffed-necked people!'" In the middle of all this, I gave three interviews: TV, radio, and print. It's all in a day's work. Say what you want about the issue of marriage equality—for or against—all politics is religious *whenever* the topic comes up for discussion.

First, let's consider the language: I don't call it "same-sex" marriage. Calling it "same-sex" marriage makes "sex" stand out and distracts my listener from the real issue. Calling it "marriage equality" communicates something different: commitment and a loving bond of protection and responsibility between devoted partners. I witnessed the importance of marriage equality when I worked as a rabbi in Massachusetts. That state's highest court established this civil right for those who decide to exercise it. My experience demonstrates that marriage strengthens the bonds between committed and loving partners. It makes an important contribution to the moral fabric of our communities. It protects children, securing them in loving, stable, and nurturing homes and safeguarding them in the face of life's unknowns. Marriage equality advances the institution of traditional marriage. Marriage is private and personal, mattering only to people who decide on it and those close to them. Many same-gender couples seek the responsibilities and protections of marriage, and the state should not be getting in their way.

What a Religious Voice Contributes to the Conversation

Even though we are talking about *secular*, or *civil*, marriage, isn't it peculiar that all the opposition is *faith-driven*? You could understand the upset of the opposition if the government wanted to force them to hold same-gender ceremonies in their synagogues or churches, but no one is asking for that. After all, what right does the state have to barge into a place of worship and tell the people inside how to practice their faith? (Ahem!) Nevertheless, marriage equality opponents are pretty crafty, cloaking their religious argument in secular vestments. They carry on about "changing the definition of traditional marriage" and "redefining the institution of family." But this is nothing more than a rhetorical "fig leaf" covering their vision of moral purity, a clever attempt to conceal a religious agenda by using secular words. That's why they get so angry at people like me, religious supporters of marriage equality; we "out" them and show that their objection is religious at heart.

Opponents of marriage equality behave as if they represent all religious people. My religious support for marriage equality undermines their standing and embarrasses them. My presence says to lawmakers, "Hey, there is another faith opinion over here! They are not the only ones. You have to think of us as you write laws!" When I enter the conversation, I show that the argument is a religious one, not a secular one. The disagreement is really between those who believe God says "Yes!" and those who believe God says "No!" and *it is not for government* to figure out which religion is right. *It is for government* to establish laws that allow individuals and couples to decide and follow through on that decision in the privacy of their homes and in their religious communities. When it comes to "what God wants," it is not for any legislator to play religious umpire and decide. There's something about these private, intimate decisions that rankles folks from a certain faith perspective. They are bothered by same-gender relations, contraception, sex education, and abortion—and the "moral agency" at the center.

Moral Agency as a Value of Faith

Moral agency is a religious and legal fundamental. This is where faith and the national vision coincide. The 1973 United States Supreme Court decision in *Roe v. Wade* found a constitutional basis for a woman making a private decision about the outcome of her pregnancy. The court affirmed her moral agency: the woman knows best. And a wide spectrum of clergy agrees with this perspective: when it comes to determining the right time to have a child, it is the woman's responsibility to make up her own mind.

Many religious leaders see something wrong with abortion. On the other hand, many folks are surprised to learn that many clergy stand by the women and that there is nothing new about our support. In 1967, six years before the *Roe* decision, twenty-one New York City clergy (nineteen ministers and two rabbis) announced the formation of the Clergy Consultation Service on Abortion[1] to counsel women about pregnancy and, if requested, to provide referrals for safe and affordable abortion care. The clergy publicly listed their names, churches, and synagogues, as well as a call-in number. Yes, listing with the Consultation Service brought the clergy the possibility of job loss and jail. But they were driven to come forward by the painful pastoral care experience of counseling women and families. The clergy spoke of desperate women trying to self-abort, of women turning to whoever said they could help, and paying whatever was asked. The clergy witnessed medical catastrophes: children born injured and deformed, and women suffering permanent injury or death. For some clergy, one trip to the cemetery with a bereft family demonstrated the truth: a woman knows whether or not her pregnancy is right for her, and when she is convinced it must end, no one can decide for her or talk her out of it. When a woman knows she needs an abortion, she doesn't need a sermon from a pastor; she needs safe and affordable medical care from a qualified medical provider. Abortion care is basic medical care; every woman deserves access, as *she* determines.

After the 1973 *Roe* decision, abortion became legal and available, and the Consultation Service disbanded—after growing into a national network of fourteen hundred clergy that referred more than one hundred thousand women for safe and affordable abortion care *without a single fatality.* Looking back, we recognize how the Clergy Consultation Service honored the moral agency of any pregnant woman, whether seeking birth-at-term, adoption, or abortion. I run into network members from time to time, and they talk about what brought them to come forward. One of the original twenty-one tells a heart-wrenching story of a teen impregnated by a relative. The family came to him for help, but he had no idea where to send them and turned them away, never learning what happened. Based on the circumstances—their desperation and the limited options—he imagined the worst. He swore he'd do better when again faced with that situation, and he helped found the Consultation Service. Today this man reflects, "Her deliberation is more important to me than the status of her pregnancy. Of course her pregnancy has value. It's just that her ability to make a decision has a higher moral standing." He and his colleagues knew there was something very wrong in forcing a woman to carry her pregnancy to term over her wishes; it was immoral to insist she bear the medical risk, cost, and more. When a wanted pregnancy takes a bad turn or when a pregnancy arrives unplanned, the ethical thing—the smart and safe thing—is to ensure the woman can talk with her doctor or nurse, hear all her options, take time to deliberate, consult with trusted others as she wishes, come to her informed decision, and receive emotional and spiritual support along with the quality and affordable care that she believes to be right for her. The decision is ultimately between her and her God.

Abortion is one of the most commonly performed medical procedures in the United States, and it is tragic that many women who have abortions are all too often mischaracterized and stigmatized, their exercise of moral agency sullied. Their judgment is publicly and forcefully second-guessed by those in politics and religion who have no business entering the deliberation. The reality is that women demonstrate forethought and care; talk to them the way clergy do and witness their sense of responsibility.

Women take abortion as seriously as any of us takes any health-care procedure. They understand the life-altering obligations of parenthood and family life. They worry over their ability to provide for a child, the impact on work, school, the children they already have, or caring for other dependents. Perhaps the woman is unable to be a single parent or is having problems with a husband or partner or other kids.[2] Maybe her contraception failed her. Maybe when it came to having sex she didn't have much choice. Maybe this pregnancy will threaten her health, making adoption an untenable option. Or perhaps a wanted pregnancy takes a bad turn and she decides on abortion. It's pretty complicated. It's her business to decide on the outcome of her pregnancy—not ours to intervene, to blame, or to punish.

Clergy know about moral agency through pastoral work. Women and families invite us into their lives to listen, reflect, offer sympathy, prayer, or comfort. But when it comes to giving advice, we recognize that we are not the ones to live with the outcome;

the patient faces the consequences. The woman bears the medical risk of a pregnancy and has to live with the results. Her determination of the medical, spiritual, and ethical dimensions holds sway. The status of her fetus, when she thinks life begins, and all the other complications are hers alone to consider. Many women know right away when a pregnancy must end or continue. Some need to think about it. Whatever a woman decides, she needs to be able to get good quality medical care and emotional and spiritual support as she works toward the outcome she seeks; she figures it out. That's all part of "moral agency." No one is denying that her fetus has a moral standing. We are affirming that her moral standing is higher; *she comes first*. Her deliberations, her considerations have priority. The patient must be the one to arrive at a conclusion and act upon it. As a rabbi, I tell people what the Jewish tradition says and describe the variety of options within the faith. They study, deliberate, conclude, and act. I cannot force them to think or do differently. People come to their decisions in their own way.

People who believe the decision is up to the woman are typically called "pro-choice." "Choice" echoes what is called "moral agency," "conscience," "informed will," or "personal autonomy"— spiritually or religiously. I favor the term "informed will" because it captures the idea that we learn and decide: First, inform the will. Then exercise conscience. In Reform Judaism, for instance, an individual demonstrates "informed will" in approaching and deciding about traditional dietary rules—in a fluid process of study of traditional teaching, consideration of the personal significance of that teaching, arriving at a conclusion, and taking action. Unitarian Universalists tell me that the search for truth and meaning leads to the exercise of conscience. We witness moral agency when a member of a faith community interprets faith teachings in light of historical religious understandings and personal conscience.

I know that some religious people don't do all this spiritual "work," and they take "the easy way out." Across the Jewish spectrum, for instance, in Orthodox, Hasidic, Conservative, Reconstructionist, and Reform communities, many people just go ahead and do whatever they want, no matter what their rabbis think or say. But this is no excuse for preventing responsible people from exercising moral agency. Of course, some religious leaders reject moral agency for an automatic acceptance of dogma, creed, or an "official" understanding of the truth. They have one set way of looking at things and want everyone to follow it. They'll smear moral agency as "anything goes," "do your own thing," or "pick and choose." This is all their right. Meanwhile, you can't stop people from setting personal direction. Of course there are things we all believe are wrong, like slavery and murder. But it is conscience first in so many other areas.

The religious debate over moral agency is centuries old. The invention of the printing press, for example, put the Bible and other religious texts in the hands of the people and expanded the opportunity to read and interpret according to conscience. Some religious authorities did not take kindly to this development, and even today their successors are not at peace. They want everybody to approach the faith precisely as they do. Others welcome personal interpretation as surely as they welcome the exercise of moral agency, as when deliberating over the use of contraception or turning to abortion.

South Dakota: An Attack on Moral Agency

Previous events in South Dakota serve as an egregious example of the attempts to tamp down moral agency. In an effort to ban abortion in South Dakota, former governor Mike Rounds and the state legislature convened a task force to study abortion, which produced the "Report of the South Dakota Task Force to Study Abortion" in 2005. As far as moral agency, the task force came to two conclusions. The first conclusion had to do with the purported "personhood" of the fetus, concluding that human life begins at fertilization, when sperm meets egg—no objections were allowed per the report. The United States Supreme Court had not seen it that way in *Roe v. Wade* and in other decisions. Many faiths, including my own, view this issue pretty much as does the court. Judaism and many other groups have long affirmed that the rights and protections of personhood come only in the final stages of birthing, not sooner, and certainly not at fertilization. Claiming life begins at conception is a religious statement. It not only differs from my faith teaching, it has no basis in science. But this report turned to the "fig leaf" of secular ideas and language. It attempted to give scientific credibility to a religious perspective and took steps toward establishing that religious perspective as state law. The report encouraged the denial of moral agency by saying no one could disagree with the religious teachings of the writers.

The report's second conclusion put forward another religious idea as a challenge to moral agency—this one about the woman's purported maternal destiny. Maternal destiny builds on an assumption that, as the report states, "the intrinsic beauty of womanhood is inseparable from the beauty of motherhood."[3] In other words, it is a woman's fate to be a mother; no other life goal for her is higher or acceptable. And when a woman decides to terminate a pregnancy, as this argument astonishingly develops, she demonstrates that she has lost her sense of her proper place in the world: her role as a mother. After all, it "is so far outside the normal conduct of a mother to implicate herself in killing her own child."[4] Since, according to the report, the woman must have been duped and coerced to the point where she does not understand herself appropriately, she should not be left to her own decision; the state will barge in and decide for her. The state sought to enshrine one faith perspective about the beginning of life and the moral agency of women—that they don't have any.

I recognize that some religious leaders uphold these teachings about fetal personhood and maternal destiny. That's how they interpret the faith. While my faith has a different teaching, I don't feel a need to dispute theirs. However, it is wrong for an elected leader to attempt to establish this particular faith perspective as the law for everyone. But that's just what the South Dakota governor and the legislature tried to do by instigating ballot initiatives to ban abortion. They tried it twice, both attempts failed—for now.

I am sorry to say that degrading the moral agency of women has a longstanding tradition and continues as a common practice. For instance, the mission documents of the Southern Baptist Convention provide another example:

> The husband and wife are of equal worth before God, since both are created in God's image. The marriage relationship models the way God relates to His people. A husband is to love his wife as Christ loved the church. He has the God given responsibility to provide for, to protect, and to lead his family. A wife is to submit herself graciously to the servant leadership of her husband even as the church willingly submits to the headship of Christ. She, being in the image of God as is her husband and thus equal to him, has the God-given responsibility to respect her husband and to serve as his helper in managing the household and nurturing the next generation.[5]

When former Alabama governor Mike Huckabee, a pastor in the church, was called upon to explain that platform plank, he said that these instructions did not mean the woman is to be subordinate, not at all. It means both husbands and wives "mutually showing their affection and submission as unto the Lord." He said, "biblically, marriage is a 100-100 deal. Each partner gives 100 percent of their devotion to the other."[6] Yes, marriage requires 100 percent devotion. And, in that church's faith, the woman demonstrates devotion through submission and the man through domination. Again, they are free to live their faith as they wish in their homes and communities. Church-state separation prevents me from walking into a private religious practice and imposing my viewpoints. But there is something wrong when the tables get turned and they bring their teachings to the floor of Congress, all in an effort to impose this religious approach on folks like me, whose faith has a different approach. It's not good enough to just stifle the moral agency within their own faith—*everyone has to comply*.

Denominations Speak about Moral Agency and Abortion

Many religious denominations and bodies have official positions on public policy issues. In contrast with some religious bodies, a wide spectrum of religious groups strongly affirm the moral agency of women, even when it comes to pregnancy. I find it uplifting to consider how the leaders of so many different faiths boldly rise to appreciate the importance of the moral agency of men and women. Let's take a look at the official positions of several denominations and groups:

American Baptist Churches, USA

"Recognizing that each person is ultimately responsible to God, we encourage women and men in these circumstances to seek spiritual counsel as they prayerfully and conscientiously consider their decision."[7]

Catholics for Choice

"We affirm that the moral capacity and the human right to make choices about whether and when to become pregnant or to end a pregnancy are supported by church teachings."[8]

Central Conference of American Rabbis

"Jewish obligation begins with the informed will of every individual."[9]

Disciples of Christ

"Persons who must decide whether or not to undergo an abortion shall have the informed supportive resources of the Christian community to help them make responsible choices, and that congregations and individuals give continued full support to each person who must make such a decision, knowing that whether or not an abortion is decided the person will need the supportive assurance of God's grace and love which meaningfully can come with the Christian community."[10]

Episcopal Church

"Any proposed legislation on the part of national or state governments regarding abortions must take special care to see that individual conscience is respected and that the responsibility of individuals to reach informed decisions in this matter is acknowledged and honored."[11]

Presbyterian Church (U.S.A.)

"We affirm the ability and responsibility of women, guided by the Scriptures and the Holy Spirit, to make good moral choices."[12]

Union for Reform Judaism (Union of American Hebrew Congregations)

"We affirm our unwavering commitment to the protection and preservation of the reproductive rights of women."[13]

Unitarian Universalist Association

"[We affirm that] the right to individual conscience, and respect for human life are inalienable rights due every person; and that the personal right to choose in regard to contraception and abortion is an important aspect of these rights."[14]

United Methodist Church

"We call all Christians to a searching and prayerful inquiry into the sorts of conditions that may cause them to consider abortion.... A decision concerning abortion should be made only after thoughtful and prayerful consideration by the parties involved, with medical, family, pastoral and other appropriate counsel."[15]

A Lesson from American History

A moral earthquake shook the United States in the early twentieth century as the nation approached, entered, and ended the Prohibition era, capped in 1919 by the ratification of the Eighteenth Amendment to the United States Constitution. The Eighteenth Amendment, followed by the Volstead Act, prohibited manufacture, transport, and sale of alcohol. The amendment sought to bring an entire nation closer to a particular religious outlook of moral purity.

All sorts of people were behind Prohibition—a surprising mix of women's organizations, religious denominations, and anti-immigration groups concerned about the many new Americans in the beer business. But something went awry as Prohibition moved from the legislatures to real life, as people ignored the laws and exploited loopholes. California grape growers skirted the amendment through an exception for production, sale, and consumption of grape juice. A carve-out for Jewish and Catholic ceremonial alcohol increased participation in religious activities. Doctors honored patients' requests to prescribe legal alcohol for an array of medical conditions, including cancer, diabetes, snakebite, asthma, and dental problems—a comforting balm for the sick. Prohibition inadvertently boosted organized crime by incentivizing bootlegging: fishing boats returned to port with the catch of the day—in bottles instead of nets. Exploiters of newer modes of transportation turned roads and rails into a liquid pipeline. Law enforcement became overwhelmed in many communities, eventually giving up and looking the other way. This is what happens when the law takes the *sin* of one religion and makes it into a *crime*.

The issues over the enforcement of Prohibition reflected the reality of people's lives—turning to the law is not right, it's not smart, and it doesn't work. There's a wise saying in the legal literature of my faith: "You can't impose a restriction on a community unless the majority of the community is willing to stand for it." As we saw during Prohibition, writing religious restrictions into public policy drives undesirable behavior underground. Eventually the opportunity to impose an excise tax on alcohol sales provided enough of a political smokescreen for the repeal of Prohibition by 1933. The nation took one step back from theocracy. But the challenge of resisting religious domination still remains. When it came to Prohibition, the government did a lousy job regulating moral behavior. Here we are, all these decades later, contending with a Prohibition mentality that thinks we can outlaw moral agency! Some folks just don't give up.

"Do We Have to Do What We Want to Do?"

I am told of a newspaper cartoon picturing a classroom table with a preschooler surrounded by too many toys, games, and crafts supplies. The caption read: "Do we have to do what we want to do?"

Yes! You have to do what you want to do. Moral agency means, you must! Of course there's a world of difference between a young student overwhelmed by play options and a person facing a serious decision. Yet when it comes to making up one's mind, the response is the same: You have to do what you want to do. You are the expert in yourself. No one can make up your mind for you. You are the one to decide.

It is a far cry from the nursery school play table to the study of the Bible or the doctor-patient relationship and a medical decision. Yet the principle is the same: the person in the situation is best equipped to make a decision; each one of us interprets the faith as conscience demands. God gives a woman the capacity to become pregnant and come to her conclusion. She has to do what she wants to do. She knows what is right for herself and her family. No one else can or should make that decision for her. It is between her and her God. Moral agency is at the core of my faith and many others. All these faith-driven attacks against moral agency are attacks against the religious beliefs of others. That's why this choir has to stand up and sing.

4

Core Faith Values
Church-State Separation

New York's court of appeals is the state's highest court, as I learned as a New York City junior high school student. In a scene I never imagined as a thirteen-year-old eighth grader, I found myself in the court of appeals as a spectator when one of our best pieces of legislation—the Women's Health and Wellness Act (WHWA)—faced legal challenge. WHWA is a great law. It addressed inequalities in women's health care by requiring insurance coverage for osteoporosis exams, prescription contraceptives, and life-saving breast and cervical cancer screenings. Given that women of reproductive age pay out-of-pocket up to 68 percent more than men for medical care, WHWA took an important step forward toward parity—to the dismay of some religious groups.[1]

To be honest, these groups apparently welcomed the preventive exams and screenings. However, the contraception requirement so upset them, they threw down all kinds of arguments as the bill moved through the state legislature to the governor for signature. When the bill became law, those religious grievances morphed into legal challenges that wound up in the state's court of appeals. The courtroom filled with advocates, clergy, and lawyers for a thirty-minute heated hearing that chilly winter afternoon. Of all the arguments, one still stands out: a lawyer's words that contraception is something "the church condemns as sinful."

Judaism and many faiths have a different teaching about contraception: Intimacy between committed partners, separate and apart from having children, is potentially holy. Contraception is a moral good when advancing the bonds of a relationship. In other words, what is "sinful" in one faith can be a blessing in another. So, I sat there and said to myself, "Hey, my religion says something different. To us, it's a sin when people can't get health care, contraception, or anything else. Why should a sin for them become a crime for me? No one is forcing them to use it. Religious disputes belong to religious people, not government courts. Throw the case out and leave the law alone!" A few months later, the court unanimously rejected the appeal. Wisdom and integrity prevailed. And why not? Why should a court bless the expansion of a religious restriction, especially when many members of the restricting community don't even follow the restrictive teaching themselves? There's plenty of religious freedom in the United States, including the freedom to abstain from contraception. On the other hand, a woman should be able to get the health care she believes is right for her, regardless of what third parties think.

Ratchet up the rhetoric to 2010 and the congressional debates over health-care reform, known as the Affordable Care Act (ACA). All to the good, as ACA moved through Congress, religious leaders of many persuasions supported the promise of quality and affordable health care for millions: young adults would be allowed to stay on parents' plans, patients would benefit from greater access to preventive care, preexisting condition requirements would be removed for those with cancer, diabetes, heart disease, and more. There would be an end to dollar limits on care, and small businesses would get tax credits.

Clergy supported health-care reform because good health is a gift from God, and the people who provide the health care are God's agents of healing and comfort. As a matter of morals and faith, we affirmed that people—rich and poor—should be able get medical services. But things went very wrong when some religious folks exploited health-care reform as an opportunity to write their faith-based restrictions into the law. As the bill moved toward a vote, it became painfully clear: without faith-based abortion restrictions, there would be no health care for so many disenfranchised millions of individuals and families. Michigan congressman Bart Stupak took the lead: no abortion restriction, no reform, and tough luck for the tens of millions of uninsured. The Stupak abortion ban passed the House. In the Senate, meanwhile, ACA limped ahead under a slightly less restrictive abortion amendment sponsored by Nebraska senator Ben Nelson. Senator Nelson's restriction satisfied some opponents, but not all.

Abortion opponent Representative Dale E. Kildee of Michigan eventually supported the Nelson revision, but only after reassurance from his parish priest that the Nelson ban was strict enough to honor his religious teachings. Representative Kildee said, "I will be eighty-one years old in September. Certainly at this point in my life, I'm not going to change my mind and support abortion, and I'm not going to risk my eternal salvation."[2] He would have voted against the bill had the priest not given him a green light. Here is the problem: Representative Kildee didn't base his vote on the national well-being. It wasn't about the Constitution or his constituents. It was his self-interest; a priest's opinion of the rules for the afterlife got priority over a woman's medical needs.

It's hard to believe that a congressman brazenly admitted that a health-care reform bill needed a priest's sign-off. Who would have ever imagined that a clergy member's representation of a personal consequence—"eternal salvation"—determines whether or not millions are insured! What a challenge this presents to millions of others whose faith teachings affirm that the outcome of a pregnancy should be left to the woman, her doctor, and trusted others to decide! Meanwhile, Representative Kildee and others take it for granted that secular law must enforce their faith restrictions, to the exclusion of all others. What a challenge to the boundary against religious infringement!

Back to Representative Stupak, who flatly refused to accept the less severe Nelson revision, even after a group of nuns joined Representative Kildee's priest and said it was okay. Representative Stupak got his orders elsewhere: "With all due respect to the nuns, when I deal or am working on right-to-life issues, we don't call the nuns. I mean, we deal with right-to-life. We deal with the U.S. Conference of Catholic Bishops."[3] Representative Stupak gave the bishops final word on federal legislation—not the United States Constitution, the Bill of Rights, or the Declaration of Independence, not doctors, and not nurses. Not even the woman in need. Only the bishops could judge whether a federal law stood religious muster. That's how Representative Stupak said our government should run its business, like a religious denomination—*his*!

Bad things happen when clergy and policy makers play doctor and force the government into the private medical decisions and care of patients of all faiths and persuasions. The Nelson ban needlessly expanded the federal bureaucracy, establishing a second and unnecessary insurance plan in the federal health insurance exchanges. Under this proposal, a woman writes two checks: one for her abortion care and one for everything else, with all the additional bookkeeping for her and the federal exchanges—another unnecessary layer of paperwork! It's hard to believe that religious pluralism like that in the United States, with a long and admirable history of protecting diverse faiths, is embracing religious restrictions. To think that policy makers would jeopardize all reform of health care—the needs of so many uninsured and sick—to put their personal faith and spiritual destinies first! As health-care reform, they want one nation under (their) God.

President John F. Kennedy and the 1960 Campaign

Senator Edward Kennedy was a longtime champion of health-care reform, frequently calling for the kinds of things ultimately included in ACA, which became in some ways his legacy. Health-care reform also brings us to consider his brother, the late

President John Kennedy, for his resistance to religious influence. During the 1960 presidential campaign, people worried that then Senator John Kennedy, a Roman Catholic, would allow the Vatican and church leaders to commandeer his decisions as president. People said he would favor his faith over others. In a landmark speech, then Senator Kennedy promised otherwise, saying:

> I believe in an America that is officially neither Catholic, Protestant nor Jewish—where no public official either requests or accepts instructions on public policy from the Pope, the National Council of Churches or any other ecclesiastical source—where no religious body seeks to impose its will directly or indirectly upon the general populace or the public acts of its officials....
>
> Whatever issue may come before me as President—on birth control, divorce, censorship, gambling or any other subject—I will make my decision in accordance with these views, in accordance with what my conscience tells me to be the national interest, and without regard to outside religious pressures or dictates.[4]

ACA honors the legacy of Senator Ted Kennedy. As for his brother's legacy of separating religion and policy, that's another story.

Why doesn't someone stop this? Where are the courts? What happened to church-state separation? Isn't anyone watching? The reality is that while we were respecting church-state separation, others planned and worked to challenge it. They believe that the Constitution, laws, and policies must conform to their faith. If they hear that the Bible calls for capital punishment, they do, too. If the book of Genesis says the world is fewer than six thousand years old, that's what we teach kids in science class. They got organized and funded, got lawyers, and got elected. Now they are working to make everyone in the country come closer to living by their religious beliefs.

Incremental Attacks on the Wall of Separation

None of us would be happy to have the microphone cut in the middle of a speech, but that's what happened to class valedictorian Brittany McComb at graduation ceremonies of Foothill High School in Henderson, Nevada. School officials turned off the power when she instructed her captive audience to convert to her faith.[5] Graduates, their families, and friends found themselves hearing a valedictorian-speech-turned-sermon promising God's love, which "is something we all desire, it's unprejudiced, it's merciful, it's free, it's real, it's huge and it's everlasting." When Brittany said, "God's love is so great that He gave up his only son," along with a graphic account of Jesus's crucifixion, the school cut the power. After all, students from many different denominations and religions attend public schools. Church-state separation makes school officials responsible for providing a podium free from religious coercion. Kids are especially prone to peer and administrative pressure; administrators have a special obligation to protect the young. Religious indoctrination is the role of the home and the faith community, not the place of the public school. That's why they cut the mic.

Newly minted graduate Brittany went home and went much further. She got a lawyer and sued, claiming her alma mater had violated her constitutional rights to speak freely. When a three-judge federal panel found in the school's favor and against Brittany's proselytizing, her lawyer went to the United States Supreme Court and filed *McComb v. Crehan*. This legal battle didn't have to be. School officials reviewed Brittany's original prepared text and approved it, even with two references to "the Lord," nine to "God," and one to "Christ." Officials agreed that she could *describe her faith* but warned her against *encouraging anyone to join it*—a perfectly reasonable approach. Let's say a Jewish teen speaks at a high school graduation. It's appropriate for her to discuss the impact of bat mitzvah, religious school and confirmation experiences, and the personal spiritual benefits in home religious observance. It's fine to describe, but *it is wrong to use a public podium to encourage, threaten, or coerce anyone to convert.* It's fine to wear a Star of David around the neck, a Jewish mystical kabbalah bracelet on the wrist, and a menorah pin on the lapel, but the public school podium is not the place to attempt to convince anyone else to do the same. When the valedictorian of Foothill High School strayed from the approved text and called folks to join her in faith, the school rightfully cut the power.

Religious people have plenty of opportunity to believe, practice, and preach. We have freedom of expression at home, in religious places, and in *most* public places, too. We can speak, carry signs, and more. But it's different in a public school, where, even on a good day, vulnerable kids already suffer under peer pressure and coercion, despite the best efforts of many caring teachers and administrators. Of course, students may study, pray, and meditate on faith during private time, but the school must not sponsor prayer or sermons or distribute prayers to recite. Students may read the Bible in class on their own, and the Bible may be taught academically as any classic text, as part of a literature or history lesson, but the school must not pressure anyone to adopt a faith. Teachers can *teach about religion*, but they may not *impose*.

America is exceptional for safeguarding the public forum from religious pressures, particularly when it comes to impressionable children. Even so, there are many who would turn the schools into a conversionary institution. This perspective dishonors the First Amendment to the Constitution, which outlaws the endorsement of faith by government and protects religion from government meddling. The First Amendment maintains, "Congress shall make no law respecting an establishment of religion, or prohibiting the free exercise thereof; or abridging the freedom of speech, or the press; or the right of people peaceably to assemble and to petition the Government for a redress of grievances." The First Amendment establishes a wall of separation between church and state, a promise that government—all arms of government, including schools, courts, libraries, the military, and more—will neither promote religious behavior nor reasonably interfere with it. Federal, state, and local governments will not play religious favorites, nor will they elevate one religious viewpoint over others. The public forum is impartial.

Church-state separation limits religious displays and behavior in courtrooms, hospitals, the military, and public schools. It means that no court or school sends the message, "You better believe this and follow these rules in order to get fair treatment here." But, as with any other issue, some religious people—growing more influential with each day—disagree and are taking on the fight. Detractors claim—correctly, in my view—that the phrase "wall of separation between church and state" appears nowhere in the United States Constitution, Bill of Rights, or Declaration of Independence. "Separation between church and state" turned up in a letter from President Thomas Jefferson dated January 1, 1802. President Jefferson wrote, "Religion is a matter which lies solely between Man and his God, that he owes account to none other for his faith or his worship ... I contemplate with sovereign reverence that act of the whole American people which declared that their legislature should," and he quotes from the Bill of Rights, "make no law respecting an establishment of religion, or prohibiting the free exercise thereof," continuing in his own words, "building a wall of separation between Church and State."[6] The *phrase* is not in the Constitution, but the *idea* is sure there. President James Madison, another founder, emphasized this point, writing in his *Detached Memoranda*: "The Constitution of the U.S. forbids everything like an establishment of a national religion."[7]

Detractors claim that the Constitution is a religious document, designed to establish the nation's Christian foundation—and they are wrong. In truth, the Constitution is a secular document. It contains no mention of Moses, Jesus, or Muhammed. It doesn't reference the Bible or purported "Judaeo-Christian" religions. The founders wrote of God in general, without elevating any particular view of that God. It's a generic idea of God, intended to appeal to a wide range of religious perspectives, leaving decisions about the specific religion to you and me, our hearts, homes, and places of worship.

So the "wall of separation between Church and State" is built into the Constitution, just as Presidents Jefferson and Madison said. Nevertheless, people disagree and the matter is constantly in the courts and press. Some folks are intent on pushing through the wall. They want their Bible to be the blueprint for everything we do—with family, in government, the arts, education, health-care law, and elsewhere. They want our laws to conform to their understanding of the alleged religious intentions of the founders and the documents they produced. They are working to enshrine their vision of cultural purity as the national brand, to bring their understanding of God's law to us all. And they are often meeting with success.

From the Reform synagogue I attended as a kid to churches and synagogues today, many of us are proud to maintain a firm church-state boundary, even while others challenge the line. When it came to *McComb v. Crehan*, the Supreme Court declined to review the case; the school administration decision stood. But when it came to health-care reform, religious forces made their sins crimes for all. All these robust challenges to church-state separation are catching us off guard; we expected everyone to respect the faith-government boundaries underpinning the national fabric. Instead, we are confronted by those who deny religious pluralism and demand that church and state are fused. What to do?

Finding a New Way to Defend Church-State Separation

An effective response begins with a clear and fresh message. You'll note that even though the Constitution establishes a barrier of separation of church and state, I avoid using this phrase. That goes back to an experience of getting pulled into a community flap over a religious holiday display in a public square, an ugly memory that includes park commission hearings, media, and more. In the midst of the fray, one of the lawyers in the congregation left me a packet of legal documents proving that a semipermanent religious display has no place on public property. I started reading but had a terrible time understanding them. (I don't have a problem understanding religious law books—say, the Talmud, even though it is written in ancient Aramaic—but something about federal appellate court decisions is different.) When another lawyer asked me what was going on, I told him about the packet of documents. He gave me some great counsel: "You're a rabbi, not a lawyer, so you're not going to give out any legal advice. Speak from your perspective as a religious leader. Tell us what you think best serves the community."

It was a defining moment for me. "Oh," I responded, "you mean, I'm not going to carry on about 'separation of church and state'— that's law. Speaking from my perspective as a community leader, I should say something like, 'We serve everyone best when we keep private religious symbols off public property. In neighborhoods like ours, where people of so many different faiths live together in peace, we help the common good by keeping the faith in our homes and in our places of worship and keeping the public square out of religion.'" That experience taught me to get away from the slogan and get into the concept. I had to stop speaking as a constitutional lawyer and start speaking as a community leader. I needed to explain, from my clergy perspective, what church-state separation means.

So I started recognizing that religious people have a special responsibility to step up. Clergy and faithful are first responders. We are in an ideal position to oppose the fusion of faith and state. You might think clergy want religion all over the place, but no! We reject efforts to establish the supremacy of one particular religious worldview to the exclusion of all others. Religious leaders present an unexpected argument for church-state separation. We surprise the public and get noticed and heard.

I also started affirming the spiritual goodness in religious freedom and tolerance. Our nation is blessed with a long history of religious protection, of honoring privacy over what to believe, where to pray, how to practice, where to give our money, and what to teach our children. As a result, the country enjoys thriving and diverse religious communities—places of worship, programs of religious education, youth organizations, summer camps, seminaries, benevolent organizations, and more. Everyone benefits when government keeps out of religion and religion keeps out of government. Yet many religious groups are challenging the wisdom of government neutrality.

I recommend making the debate about religion in public life because "the wall of separation between church and state" has become a cliché, more of a lightning rod than a useful term. Talking about church-state separation doesn't work well anymore; it only gives opponents an opening to get their point across. It's better to put the phrase aside and adopt more precise ideas and language that describe the proper role of government toward religious life, how faith stands in relation to government, and the consequences of violating the boundary between the two. Here are some ways to open the conversation; more specifics later, when we get to "message triangles" and "talking points." Begin with language like this:

- The government is not to play religious favorites.
- Passing a law doesn't make something moral.
- We don't elect senators to referee religious disagreements.
- We love this country for its religious freedoms and protections.
- It breaks my heart to legislate religious restrictions into law.
- You can't force an entire Untied States to honor the teachings of one religion.
- The United States protects religious freedoms in a way that makes us the envy of the world.
- America is exceptional for church-state separation.
- It's only fair to let people follow their faith in peace.
- Congress oversteps its authority by deciding among religions.

Let's take a look at some nationally endorsed denominational statements on the topic:

American Baptist Churches

"We proclaim that separation of church and state is central to our American heritage; that it has made possible a measure of freedom not previously achieved under any other system; that it is indispensable to our national policy of equal rights for all religions and special privileges for no religion."[8]

Evangelical Lutheran Church in America

"[We] work with civil authorities in areas of mutual endeavor, maintaining institutional separation of church and state in a relation of functional interaction."[9]

Union for Reform Judaism (Union of American Hebrew Congregations)

"The Union of American Hebrew Congregations has, throughout its history, steadfastly maintained the principle of separation of church and state, believing that the First Amendment to the Constitution is the bulwark of religious freedom and interfaith amity."[10]

Unitarian Universalist Association

"Be it resolved: That the Unitarian Universalist Association at its 1963 General Assembly, reaffirms its support of religious freedom based on the principle of separation of church and state and urges its members to:

- Uphold the principle of non-sectarian public education;
- Oppose Bible readings and religious observances in the public schools;
- Oppose released time for religious education;
- Refrain, if possible, from holding religious services or classes on public property;
- Refrain from use of public school property for such purposes without payment of a fair rental;
- Oppose shared time in public schools;
- Pay a full and fair market price for church building sites in publicly subsidized urban renewal areas and refuse to locate where a city, a state, or a federal subsidy is either implicit or explicit."[11]

United Methodist Church

"[The] government may not engage in, sponsor, supervise, aid, or lend its authority to religious expressions or religious observances.

- Be it further resolved, that the General Conference urge rejection of any attempt of legislative bodies at the federal and state levels to bridge this important separation between church and state by providing direct financial assistance to houses of worship and religiously affiliated organizations in order for them to evangelize or proselytize. The state should not support any religious group's interest to evangelize or proselytize, the state is not the defender of the faith, whichever that faith might be.

- Be it further resolved, that the General Conference reaffirms its historical position in opposition to any government legislation or constitutional amendment that would allow the use of public funds to support nonpublic elementary and secondary schools, or in regards to religious observances in public schools." [12]

United Synagogue of Conservative Judaism

"[The United Synagogue] opposes all forms of organized public prayer, religious exercises or sectarian Bible classes in primary and secondary public schools, including 'moments of silence or meditation' by which prayer is expressly or implicitly encouraged or recommended; it being the firm position of United Synagogue of Conservative Judaism that prayer, religious experiences, and religious education are the responsibilities of the home, the synagogue, and other places of worship; and be it further resolved, that the United Synagogue of Conservative Judaism opposes the public funding or display on public grounds of religious symbols which imply public support of religious doctrines." [13]

Equal Treatment for All

Again, this is not about proving the other religion is wrong. Perhaps they read the Bible incorrectly or rely on a bad translation of the original Hebrew. They are nevertheless entitled to their faith, no matter how much it contradicts mine. That's what we really mean by moral agency and church-state separation: each of us has every right to be mistaken. After all, this is a democracy.

Any religious leader is graced to preach to the faithful in places of worship, to inform the public about faith practices and moral perspectives, to invite others to enter the fold, and to welcome them when and if they decide to join. Proving folks wrong went out with the Middle Ages. So when it comes to church-state separation, I take a positive approach; all religious people look bad when we go negative. At the end of the day, laws must ensure equal treatment for people of all faiths and freedom from government intrusion. Of course, it's a cause for grave concern that some people are enshrining their interpretation of the Bible as the foundation for our national vision and direction. They are brazen. We tend to be complacent. So the choir has to sing, now!

Part II

How to Speak about Religious Values

5

Messaging
to the Base

The first part of *All Politics Is Religious* explored the relationships of faith and policy. It identified core religious values: justice and mercy; caring for the widow, the stranger, and the orphan; moral agency; and church-state separation. It defined our audience as ourselves and those on the cusp of joining us. It showed the high stakes and the urgency of the problem. This second part offers language and methods of bold and respectful speech. It provides ideas and words that stir emotion and encourage people to act. Let's turn to the conversation in the aftermath of the passage of health-care reform as an example how we can begin to have respectful dialogue.

Watching Out for Mischaracterization— and Writing a Compelling Sermon

The Affordable Care Act (ACA), also known as national health-care reform, got labeled "Obamacare" by detractors, who smeared the bill with the name of someone they disliked. Many supporters of the act allowed that smear to go unchallenged—sometimes even using the language themselves—to national detriment. When speaking faith, begin by overturning mischaracterization—don't let them get away with it.

2/21/14

The reality is that health-care reform had less to do with President Obama than opponents would like to admit. ACA included provisions he didn't want (such as abortion restrictions) and lacked benefits he sought (like a public health insurance option under a government umbrella). Health-care reform came out different than the president intended; it's misleading to name it after him. ACA wasn't one guy's volley; health-care reform was the product of a constitutional, legal government process. So let's clear the air by saying, "This conversation is not about the president. It is about the need for quality and affordable health care for all who live here. Let's talk about health care."

In another example of the use of language to achieve a political end, look at the term "illegal immigration." People use it so often, you'd think it's one word. It saddens me that highly reputable media professionals have fallen for this ruse, too. The reality is that the majority of immigrants are in this country legally. They work and pay taxes, some paying more in taxes than they will ever receive in benefits. Immigrants work legally on farms, where they pick and pack the fruits and vegetables most Americans eat. They work legally in restaurant kitchens preparing our meals; the relaxing lunch or dinner out for us can mean the difference between an immigrant family surviving here or not. Other immigrants serve our nation legally and honorably in the armed forces. And, as a baseball fan, I can tell you that there are many immigrants on the ballfield. People in the grandstand carry on about managers, umpires, and player performance. But no one complains about the immigrant slugger at the plate. Nobody yells at him for not learning English or grouses over the cost of providing an English-language interpreter. As long as he gets a hit and catches the ball, no one cares. If he's really good, they put his name up in the Hall of Fame, immigrant or not. The point is that any conversation about immigration has to include the many immigrants who are here under the law, as tax-paying, productive members of society.

What is more, "illegal immigrant" is inaccurate. An "illegal" immigrant is in this country without documents, so the term "undocumented immigrant" is more appropriate. It's the same when someone drives without a license—he is not an "illegal driver," but an "unlicensed driver." And please don't accuse them all of "border jumping." Many immigrants came to the United States under the law through work, study, or travel visas. They became "undocumented" when the visa expired and they stayed. Maybe they wanted to go home but ran out of money and couldn't pay for the return. Perhaps a health crisis or a family emergency got in the way. Whatever the reason, a person lacking legal papers is not an "illegal" person, but here without papers—that is, "undocumented." The crime, if there is one, is a civil crime, more like a speeding ticket than a criminal act like ax murder or armed robbery. The issue of undocumented immigration does not deserve the vitriol it receives.

Let's look at the logistics of deporting the estimated ten million undocumented immigrants. Deporting three thousand a day makes for one million a year. Even at that breakneck and unreachable rate, it would take a decade and cost a fortune to do the job. So let's tone down the rhetoric, come up with reasonable, fair, and responsible immigration reform that also safeguards national security and protects the folks who were born here or became citizens under the law. And let's be more careful when choosing words.

We have a lot of work to do, and we can start by calling people on language. It's "health-care reform," not "Obamacare." An immigrant is not "illegal," though perhaps "undocumented." Many more immigrants are in the United States legally, working hard, paying taxes, serving in the military, and contributing to the well-being of our communities and the nation. Clarity of communication and a focus on the issues, getting away from attacking people and dealing with the matter at hand, are ways to begin speaking about faith and policy.

When it comes to preaching on difficult topics, you have two sermons right there, based on an effective strategy of cleaning up the strident rhetoric—one sermon on health care and the other on immigration. Your issue is the language—not the issue itself and not the people who use the language. You are not demonizing any elected leader or public figure, and you are not blaming any political party or religious group. You are respectfully calling your audience or congregation to accurate speech. No one can rightfully fault you for contributing a measure of respect to the conversation. Thus we start our study of dialogue by minding the content and tone of speech. Now, we turn to the methods of communication used by folks who take positions that differ from mine.

Recognizing "Dog Whistle" Messaging

It was one of my first assignments. "Study how the religious right communicates," I heard as I began my new job as an advocate. "Figure out their internal messaging. Learn how they talk to their own."

It's obvious, I thought. They say outrageous things. Their supporters cheer and send them money. They go out and say more outrageous things. Their supporters cheer and send even more money. And on Election Day, every one of their supporters goes out to vote. But who wants to be Mr. Smarty Pants on a new job? I sat there, listened, and didn't speak a word. Time passed and I learned. On the one hand, I was right. They say outrageous things and their supporters rally. I learned how they talk to their own.

Take Senator Jon Kyl (R-Arizona). He got it upside down and backward when he told the U.S. Senate that abortion is "well over 90 percent of what Planned Parenthood does." The reality is that "well over 90 percent of what Planned Parenthood does" has nothing to do with abortion. Planned Parenthood provides annual exams, cancer screenings, contraception, sex education for teens, and more. When questioned on this, the senator's office said the remarks were "not intended to be a factual statement."[1] My take says the senator wasn't interested in facts; all he wanted was rhetoric. I can almost hear his followers say, "Good for him for having the nerve to speak his mind!" It made no difference whether he was wrong, right, or got some numbers reversed. He defined his audience: Planned Parenthood opponents. He said whatever he wanted and successfully rallied his supporters. Senator Kyl was messaging to the base.

2/4/14

Public figures misstate and exaggerate to motivate their prime supporters. They cajole, blame the victim, and twist their theology to suit their purposes and message to their base. For instance, I cringe when a pastor proclaims that a hurricane is a punishment from God, even as survivors search for loved ones in the rubble and mud. I think, How callous can a religious leader be? You would think he'd offer a word of compassion for the dead and the suffering! He's giving all clergy a bad name. He should be expressing sympathy for the victims, including them in prayer, and offering help. Meanwhile, his faithful rally around his outlandish message. Or I'll read about some rabbi's rant that a spiritual failure of the fallen brought on the Nazi Holocaust, and I am outraged. Think of all the innocent people who died! Where does this guy come off? What about all the religious folks who perished in the concentration camps? Meanwhile, that rabbi's followers cry out, "Amen!" This is how a certain brand of religious leader communicates. Office holders do the same thing: warping the truth to fit a predetermined conclusion.

People call this kind of communication "dog whistle" messaging. A real dog whistle sounds a frequency that dogs hear but is too high for people. A dog whistle message speaks "code" that stirs up the political base but puzzles, angers, or goes right over the head of an outsider like me. Insiders understand it; others are left out. Dog whistle messaging uses language to provoke emotions that drive action like voting, volunteering, and donating. In case you are wondering, I own a dog whistle, too. We will get to that in a bit. First, let's try to hear the whistle of those who take stands that differ from mine. Here are some examples:

- The minister says, "the culture of life," "the seamless web of life," or "pro-life." The choir hears that abortion is a sin and wants their sin to become against the law for all, and the congregation responds with a soulful "Amen."
- The senator champions "small government," "balanced budget," and "no new taxes." The electorate hears holding the poor accountable for poverty, making the unemployed responsible for being out of work, and all victims blamed.

- The congresswoman proclaims "traditional marriage between one man and one woman." The audience hears bias against gays and rises to agree.
- A political commentator blasts that "President Obama wasn't born in the United States." The followers hear that he should not be president because he is not one of us, a stranger.

The dog whistle is a rhetorical tool with a long and painful history. The late Alabama governor George Wallace used a dog whistle when he spoke about "segregation." Everyone knew he was talking about race, but no one could pin him down. He whistled his tune and almost got away with it.[2] In his 1963 inaugural speech, he proclaimed, "I say segregation today, segregation tomorrow, segregation forever. The true brotherhood of America, of respecting the separateness of others." After wrapping his ideas in the American flag, he went on: "We invite the Negro citizens of Alabama to work with us from his separate racial station to develop, to grow in individual freedom and enrichment. We want jobs and a good future for BOTH races."

Sounds generous—everyone wins with races apart. It's patriotic, and like all politics, it's religious. He continued, "This is the basic heritage of my religion, for we are all the handiwork of God." And people who disagree are among our greatest enemies: "But we warn those, of any group, who would follow the false doctrine of communistic amalgamation that we will not surrender our system of government, our freedom of race and religion—that freedom was won at a hard price and if it requires a hard price to retain it, we are able, and quite willing to pay it." Of course, he closed with a word to God: "And my prayer is that the Father who reigns above us will bless all the people of this great sovereign State and nation, both white and black."

As Governor Wallace turned his attention from the Alabama state house to the White House, he'd lambaste "over-educated, ivory tower folks who want to tax the working man to pay people not to work and not to burn our cities down," and his loyalists knew who he meant.[3] He pointed to "the breakdown of law and order" as a national crisis, and folks flocked to his cause.[4] Governor Wallace maintained that folks of different colors need to be apart, and he added a dose of patriotism and a spoonful of religion to drive home his point. "Segregation today, segregation tomorrow, segregation forever" worked like a dog whistle, resonating within the audible emotional spectrum of supporters. He threw a meaty bone to his base, while throwing the outsider off balance: we see through the euphemism, but can't get a handle on it.

There is nothing new about using clever language to arouse images and stir emotions, leaving outsiders behind. It can even make bigotry look generous when it carries on about the nobility of keeping races apart, but all the while the unspoken intention is to keep people down. In his later years, Governor Wallace distanced himself from his thinly hidden intentions: "I made a mistake in the sense that I should have clarified my position more." He added, "I also was never saying anything that reflected on black people, and I am very sorry it was taken that way." He eventually apologized to civil rights leaders: "I'm sorry."[5] He knew he was playing games with words and playing on emotions about race. Race stirs powerful feelings. So does gender.

A successful election campaign demands a pinpointed audience and message. Identifying a proper bloc of "swing voters" and sending that bloc the right words can make or break an election. The 2000 presidential campaign found everyone messaging to "Soccer Mom"—a stereotyped worried, indecisive woman concerned with the financial future of her family. Soccer Mom worked part-time or was a "stay at home" mother. She drove a minivan as a family taxi, shuttling kids between school, soccer games, music lessons, and home. Soccer Mom fretted: Can we afford steak instead of Hamburger Helper? Can we have a Disney vacation instead of a week with the in-laws? Can we pay for the orthodontist, save for college, and put a few dollars more away for retirement? Soccer Mom decided her vote based on how she saw her family faring. If the household budget is balanced, she goes for the incumbent. If family finances are headed south and Dad's job security is uncertain, she votes for the challenger. Candidates and their staff tailored their message—ads, speeches, promotional calls—to stir Soccer Mom to action. After all, she was the swing vote in a close election. The national destiny was in her hands!

Things changed after the September 11, 2001, terror attacks: Soccer Mom became "Security Mom." She was already worried about family finances, and as the 2004 elections approached, national security joined her list, so campaigns fine-tuned the message. By 2008, former Alaska governor Sarah Palin turned Security Mom into a more decisive "Hockey Mom." The minivan, already filled with kids, now burst with ice skates, helmets, clubs, and pucks—all for a 5:00 a.m. battle on ice, with Hockey Mom (the lipsticked pit bull) cheering in the stands. The Hockey Mom identity turned audience and message into one, eventually morphing into "Momma Grizzly," fanged and clawed, poised to attack anyone who messes with the cubs.

President Ronald Reagan also worked an image to move an audience. His characterization of the "welfare queen" contributed to some of the most effective stump speeches ever: "There's a woman in Chicago. She has 80 names, 30 addresses, 12 Social Security cards and is collecting veterans' benefits on four nonexising [sic] deceased husbands. And she's collecting Social Security on her cards. She's got Medicaid, getting food stamps and she is collecting welfare under each of her names. Her tax-free cash income alone is over $150,000."[6]

President Reagan used these words in community after community, leaving plenty of anger in his wake. He offered a subliminal message about a range of emotionally troubling issues, including public assistance, gender, race, the work ethic, poverty, and the efficiency of government. The "welfare queen" was a dog whistle message describing the irresponsible and lazy moocher, clever enough to game the system instead of holding a job like everyone else. In the mind of the listener, the welfare queen took advantage of hard-working taxpayers, living easy off the sweat of others. She symbolized a government that was a careless steward of the people's treasure, a wasteful bureaucracy that squanders limited resources by rewarding bad behavior. Never mind that "welfare queen" was a bad example of a serious problem, that there were—and are still—many deserving people in great need. It gave public assistance opponents a pretext for blaming the victim. It offered an excuse to attack the social safety net, rip it to shreds, and deny people with legitimate needs. The image of the "welfare queen" helped make Ronald Reagan president of the United States.

So who was she? No one ever knew. President Reagan never referred to her by name. The Chicago papers pointed to a woman named Linda Taylor, who was eventually convicted of fraud and perjury, but no one was certain. Linda Taylor was found to be using two aliases, not eighty as President Reagan maintained. She collected twenty-three public assistance checks worth $8,000, not $150,000. But, as with Senator Kyl, accuracy doesn't matter. Identity, numbers, and reality have no bearing on the conversation as long as the image sticks.

The image of the welfare queen was a consummate dog whistle message. President Reagan never explicitly had to say she was black or poor, and he didn't harp on her gender. He didn't need to single out the employee or the government department at fault. He didn't have to put those thoughts into words. The people understood. And he didn't apologize to the electorate for describing someone who, for all we know, existed only in his mind. None of this mattered any more than it did when Senator Kyl carried on about Planned Parenthood. When it comes to angry people, facts are irrelevant; only emotions count.

Before we move on, let's acknowledge how exasperating and painful it is to drag through this conversation of economics, race, and gender. It's frightening to witness this ugly interplay of politics, communication, and emotion. How can we use what we have learned?

My New Approach to Preaching and Writing

As the dust settled after the 2000 national election and again after 2004, recrimination passed among many supporters of the defeated Democratic candidates. We blamed ourselves for the loss, convinced that had we used better, more compelling language, we would have earned more votes and perhaps achieved a different outcome. I came into this conversation as the 2004 election approached, beginning my new career as an advocate. This book is my attempt to speak to the issues. This is what I did: *I got a new whistle.*

In the past, I'd lump people and ideas together by using well-recognized terms. I'd rail against the "religious right" or attack "Republicans" and "conservatives." I'd trumpet a "progressive" agenda and rely on quotes from sympathetic public figures to make my argument. Many of us use this style of speech as a shortcut to a quick picture of where a person or situation stands—and that's a mistake. These terms stir the wrong emotions and bring folks to the wrong conclusions. My audience typecast me as a "liberal" and either dismissed or welcomed my arguments depending on where they stood. Even if people liked what I said, few did anything about it, because I wasn't giving them anything new. They lost interest by the time I preached into my second paragraph. "There he goes again!" Sure, I was correct, but I wasn't very persuasive. I was preaching to the choir in a key no one was interested in singing. My dog whistle didn't work.

So I got rid of that broken whistle; I stopped using worn-out terms. For instance, I'm really not a "liberal." Like many "conservatives," I believe in punishing criminals and in keeping taxes as low as possible. I want a strong, safe, and secure United States, and I think people should be free to live their private lives without government interference. Like many conservatives, I read the United States Constitution from time to time, the Bible almost every day, and attend regular religious worship. I vote, pay taxes, and take pride in my relatives' service in the armed forces. Let's look at people from "religious right" denominations who are not at all "conservative." Many Roman Catholic and Evangelical clergy will say to a woman, "Yes, we teach that abortion is a sin. But God loves you, no matter what you believe you should do. Just make sure you get good medical care." Sometimes they will even add, "Here's a number to call. You can trust the people there." Then we have abortion opponents who are—surprise—among staunch supporters of teaching evolution in public schools and leaving Bible lessons to church. Some who condemn contraception will accept war as a last resort, and, unlike many others on the religious right, oppose capital punishment under any circumstance.

The reality is that the jargon we commonly use to describe people, their beliefs, and affiliations is imprecise, vague, and doesn't communicate all that much. Catchalls like "left" and "right" don't catch all; instead, they stir emotions like boredom that lead to inaction or anger. So I put down that old dog whistle and got rid of the old songs. I stopped using stereotypes and turned to new music that the choir can sing.

I Started Appealing to Emotion

Most clergy eventually learn that emotions communicate better than ideas. We are more effective communicators when conveying *feelings, not facts*. We generally don't learn it in seminary; I learned from experience, as I saw most pointedly when officiating at life-cycle events: baby namings, weddings, and particularly funerals. When I first started as a rabbi, it was just the facts, nothing but. I'd get a call for a funeral, sit down with a bereft family, and learn as many details as possible. I got a full life history of the deceased, starting with early childhood, education, career, family, friends, and more. When I sat down to write a eulogy, I put as many facts as possible into my remarks. While this "did the job," I always came away from the funeral service feeling that there was something missing, that there was more to say.

As time passed, I started placing less focus on the details and more attention on the bigger picture. I started capping a eulogy with a warm or humorous story or with a description of a situation that exemplified a central feature of the personality. I still sit down with a family, listen just as carefully, but pay attention to different things. I ask, "Can you give me examples that capture his spirit?" One family told of a man who made friends as a five-year-old and continued to make friends throughout life; his life theme was community. Another was of a mother who walked her kids to school each morning and stood by her family through great challenges; her theme was devotion. For a married person, I'd ask a surviving spouse, "Tell me how you met?" "Tell me why you thought this relationship was right?" I would include these responses in the eulogy and found myself evoking feelings that spoke to what it was like to really know the person. I can't make the grief go away, but I can portray a life theme that engages people and, I hope, brings comfort. What is true for communicating about people is also true when it comes to communicating about policy.

A compelling presentation needs hard facts, but too many facts get in the way. For instance, when I say that abortion is one of the most commonly performed medical procedures in the United States, people are likely to remember. But when they hear a true story about a woman who died because she couldn't get safe care, they will remember the feelings they experienced when they heard that story and become more likely to take action. People aren't moved by the *information* I give them; they act on the *emotions* I arouse. There's nothing new about this kind of communication; the Hebrew Bible knew this, too. Let's look at two examples.

Had the Hebrew Bible said, "Don't murder!" and left it at that, perhaps the point would have gotten through and the teaching would have endured. But the Bible goes further, illustrating the significance of this lesson with the vivid narrative of the first recorded murder, when Cain kills Abel. Immediately after Abel's death, God asks Cain, "Where is your brother Abel?" And Cain responds, "I don't know. Am I my brother's keeper?"

And God responds, "What have you done? The voice of your brother's blood is crying at me from the earth! Now, you are cursed by the earth that opened its mouth to take your brother's blood from your hands. When you work the earth, it will not give you its yield. You will be a permanent wanderer across the earth" (Genesis 4:8–12).

The Hebrew Bible provides passionate language that brings life and emphasis to the teaching. "Do not murder!" *tells* people not to take a life. But it is much more effective, more engaging, to *show* what murder does by using metaphors: the earth opening a mouth, blood crying out, and the punishment of having to wander the face of the earth in perpetuity. The Bible not only *tells* people about the law against murder. It *shows* the importance of that rule as well as the consequences of breaking it. A story stirs emotions and the lesson sticks.

The same thing happens later in Exodus. The Hebrew Bible says, "Do not make for yourself an idol any representation of what is in the heavens above and on the earth below. You shall not bow down to them or serve them" (Exodus 20:4–5). Again, a rule *tells* us: no idols, period. But the Bible doesn't leave it at that; it goes on to emphasize the significance of this teaching with a story. The Bible *shows* us: God makes and inscribes the two tablets of the Ten Commandments and gives them to Moses. Moses witnesses the sin of idol worship, and we read, "When Moses approached the camp and saw the calf and the celebration, he became furious and threw the tablets from his hands and shattered them at the mountain base" (Exodus 32:19). The story continues with a narration of God's rage, punishment, and reconciliation. It's a stirring story. Vivid language—fury, shattered tablets—is a biblical tool of driving home a lesson. That's my new whistle, my new tune.

I Stopped Preaching to the Other Choir

In my previous life, I'd aim to win folks over to my side by arguing that my opponents were wrong and I was right. I realized I was preaching to the wrong choir. I naively imagined people sitting there, listening to me carry on about environment, stem cell research, or capital punishment and suddenly say, "Gee, that rabbi is so smart! He just convinced me to change my mind! To think that I have been walking around my entire life with the wrong idea!" But people aren't made that way. We tend to be inflexible. Even the best sermons aren't very effective at swaying opposing opinions. So I stopped trying to change people. I stopped harping on the inconsistencies and mistakes of the other side. I stopped trying to convince my opponents of the errors of their ways and started talking to those who agree with me, describing what they can do and say, motivating those in agreement into action.

People are free to disagree with me. My opponents are friends, neighbors, and family members. They live in our communities, fix things in our homes, provide our medical care, and service our cars. Some of them are in our families. We love them, live near them, and work with them. They are entitled to their beliefs, and I leave them be. Now I preach to *my* choir instead of *theirs*. I spend less time in attack.

I No Longer Confuse Policy with Politics and Politicians

I rarely refer to elected leaders by name, and I avoid discussing political parties. That's because, as a religious spokesperson, I am not really that interested in the *people* holding office or the *parties* they belong to. I am interested in what my faith teaches and the *policies* our country stands for and advances. It's about what we do, not about who does it. That's the difference between *politics* on the pulpit and *policy* on the pulpit. Policy means saying, "I want clean air and that is a religious value!" Politics means saying, "I want the president to give us clean air … or else! And while we are at it, look at all the other bad things the president is doing!" Politics has less of a focus on faith. Policy means: "I want a healthy, thriving natural environment, no matter which party or individual holds public office."

I know it's tough to keep away from political discussions. Media folks, community members, and family turn just about every conversation to talk about personalities, parties, who runs for office, and speculation on who will win. These conversations stir interest and drive the audience and ratings. But the day-in, day-out of political ups and downs don't belong on the pulpit, where they only distract from the issues—like the need for children to be kept healthy and safe and given an education. As a religious leader, I want my conversations to focus on what my faith says and how our teachings inform an approach. Have the president's popularity ratings dipped or upticked again? Have the Republicans tacked right and the Democrats shifted to the center? Perhaps, but that's not the point. The point is policy.

We have now defined our audience—our own faithful—identified the issues, figured out what others did right and what we did wrong, and put some new ideas on the table. We traded in the old whistle and picked up a new one. But before we develop a compelling message, we start small and smartly by building relationships with officials and the media, the kind of relationships that Martin Buber talked about. So hold off on the letter to the editor for a little more. And let's wait on the lobby visit. Let's shift gears, lower the volume, relax a little, and think and prepare.

The next several chapters provide the nuts-and-bolts "how-to" of media and lobbying, things I should have learned in seminary but never did. It may sound strange that religious leaders have anything to learn about communications, but the lesson starts here.

6

Media Relations

First Steps

My TV debut was as a five-year-old on *Romper Room*, the live-broadcast hit for preschoolers in the days of black-and-white. The program included games, songs, and a snack of graham crackers with milk. Talking points? The presnack prayer: "God is great, God is good, let us thank Him for our food. Amen." Of course, we opened with the Pledge of Allegiance. Thanks to a preshow interview that put me at ease, I aced the debut, had fun on camera, and wasn't at all nervous, although the guys fiddling around behind the big cameras looked a little frightening.

Fast-forward, decades later. The media, like life, is way more complicated. I get nervous or at least charged up preparing for an interview, and you probably do, too. This chapter is designed to increase familiarity and comfort with the media: print, web, radio, and television. I hope it brings you some of the self-assured, happy-go-lucky feeling I had on camera as a kid. Start small by working on a press release.

The Press Release: Promoting the Work of the Faith Community

Local papers are often happy to carry a well-written press release, even for an activity you take for granted. In the larger cities, where the press takes more of a national and international focus, the editor will likely pass on an announcement of the congregation's annual covered-dish dinner. But a local weekly or website may well be willing to give it a paragraph. You can submit a release about anything—from a sermon topic to a children's program, from the opening of Sunday school to a guest speaker. Send it out and see who takes it.

These simple press releases, along with op-eds and letters to the editor, serve several purposes:

- *Attracting new people (potential members), whether or not they come to that specific event.* They'll read what you do, learn about you, and maybe attend an event in the future.
- *Educating the larger community about how your faith works.* Folks passing by the church or fellowship regularly, as well as curious neighbors, may never walk through the door but wonder what goes on inside. They may have heard odd things about your beliefs and practices. Show people what you do in there.
- *Strengthening self-respect.* Members are proud to see their church receive attention. It boosts their pride and spirit.
- *Presenting organized religion in a positive light.* Many people think that religion is filled with angry followers who go around judging everybody. They'll have to reconsider when reading about the good you do.
- *Raising the profile of the clergy member.* Media attention supports the position of the religious leader in the eyes of the congregation and community.

The press release addresses some, if not all, of these questions, whether or not the paper has carried this information in the past:

- What is happening?
- Who is sponsoring the event?
- Who does it appeal to—for instance, by age and interest?
- Where will it be?
- What makes the event significant?
- What does it cost?
- What do I bring?

- When is the date and time?
- What is the contact information? Include phone number, street address, e-mail address, and website.
- How long will the event last?
- How do I make a reservation, and by when do I need to do that?
- Where do I enter the building?

End the press release with the standard hash marks: ###. Each newspaper has its own requirements. Check the website for the following information:

- Suggested length
- How soon before the event the release must be submitted
- Submission instructions (e-mail, fax, or a form on a web page; most papers don't open attachments)

To make things easier, follow these tips:

- Take language directly from your congregational bulletin. Copy-and-paste spares the need to rewrite.
- When events are similar year to year, keep a file in the computer and recycle, carefully checking and rechecking time, date, and other details.
- Line up someone in the office or a volunteer to submit press releases on a regular basis. Review the events schedule with that person and figure out what to promote.
- If the paper wants a release ten days before an event, mark a calendar to remind you of all the deadlines.
- Proofread, proofread, and proofread. Check dates, times, and phone numbers. Check them again. Check e-mail addresses, too. The simple things are most likely to contain the errors—believe me, I know!
- There is nothing wrong with sending an identical press release to various venues. Submit to local dailies, weeklies, and websites. No one will be upset when an event announcement appears widely.

Keep security in mind. Make the decision that is right for you about publishing e-mail addresses and phone numbers. I avoid including home addresses and personal e-mails in bulk publicity; if your publicity is really working, you never know who you'll attract. Office numbers and e-mails are better suited for RSVPs or if the paper needs to call to check on a detail.

Get More Punch Out of It

For a holiday announcement, for instance, briefly describe the religious significance of the occasion. Use the release as a tool for education. Include a quote or words of reflection from yourself or someone else. This is what you call a "teachable moment." Personal remarks warm up the text. Also, consider sending a photo. Everyone wants events photographed, but few people think of bringing the camera to the event, using it, and doing anything with the pictures after. Remember to do the following:

- Get publication permission from the folks in the photo. This is especially important with children and teens.
- Write a brief caption.
- When you send a press release announcing a guest speaker, include a photo as well.

Deal with Rejection

If you can't handle rejection, then don't work with the media. Don't get angry if they pass on your piece, whether it be a press release, letter to the editor, or op-ed. Maybe it got lost. Maybe they never got it. Maybe the editor took a sick day and a sub put something else in the paper instead. If there is time for resubmission, resend and follow up immediately with a phone call to make sure it arrived. But don't give anyone a hard time, and don't be surprised if you are asked to consider paying for an advertisement. The finance side of media is more complicated and pressured than ever.

If They Make a Mistake

Read the published text carefully. It drives folks in the congregation to distraction when the paper makes an error in spelling the congregation's name or the event time. Again, don't get angry. (I wonder, *Maybe the mistake was mine!*) Check your submission copy (you saved it, right?). If there is time for publishing a correction, calmly contact the paper by phone or e-mail and ask them to make the change. Generally speaking, getting it right the first time is much better than running a correction. But when there is an error and correction to be made, you have an opportunity for a second announcement and your event gets more attention.

Letters to the Editor That Make the Cut

You might ask, "What's the big deal about writing a letter to an editor (LTE)? You read something in the newspaper you don't like, dash off a few lines, tell them how angry you are, and done is done. It's not complicated at all!" Truth is, there's an art to producing a good LTE. A good letter achieves a number of things. It raises the profile of an issue, bringing it to the attention of the public, community leaders, and decision makers. It also raises the profile of an issue in the mind of an editor, even when the letter is rejected. It calls attention that perhaps leads to future coverage or even a supportive editorial.

Imagine that a letter gets published and moves a city counselor to raise the matter with the mayor, who probably saw the letter, too. Before you know it, there is another letter or a community meeting, and a bill gets drafted, passed by committee, and comes up for a vote. Of course, many letters are read and forgotten; nevertheless it is still important to write. Nothing gets better when the choir is silent. When grumblings over the news reports never make it past the TV screen or when comments among the family don't go beyond the dinner table, an opportunity to bring a positive change is lost. You and I have to write, communicate effectively, and impress the people who make the decisions. We have to use the little time we are allotted to grab the attention of a busy, besieged editor as well as the reader, who may be racing to the sports or finance section over breakfast before jumping in the car for the ride to school or work.

Before writing your LTE, check the publication's website for instructions:

- How many words is the maximum? Generally, LTEs top out at 150 words, though there are exceptions. My favorites are zingers of two or three sentences.
- Do they consider multiple submissions? If they do and you send the letter elsewhere, make sure all the editors know.
- Do they send you a rejection e-mail or do they just let it die?
- How is the LTE submitted (e-mail, fax, or through a web link)? Most papers don't open attachments.
- Must a letter respond to an article? Or is the letter page more like an open discussion forum? Some papers allow both.
- What contact information is required? The paper may want to call to confirm that you really sent it.
- If you are responding to an article, how many days do you have for submission? If time allows, write the letter, e-mail it to yourself, sleep on it, review it, and *then* send it out.
- How long will you have to wait before sending another letter? This is important if you are writing about something controversial and feel you need to respond to a responder. Some papers have a thirty- or sixty-day wait until they consider another letter from the same person. I generally don't respond to LTEs that criticize something I have written. I just assume my LTE will not be the last word and make my peace with it.
- What is the policy on placing letters on the website? Are some letters web only? Are all letters both?
- How much editing will they do? Will they let you know about changes?

Have a Good Opening

Your piece needs to jump out and get to the top of the pile. The opening must be a clincher; it's the most important part of the letter. Editors get plenty of mail and often make a decision based on the first words, leaving little leeway to grab an editor's attention and become one of the four or five out of twenty-five or more that makes it. How many times do I breeze through the morning paper only to have someone at the office ask, "Did you read that interesting letter about the rise in gasoline prices?" I looked right over it. Or if I read it, I have trouble remembering what it said. Some of that has to do with me—too much to keep in my mind. But some of it has to do with the article or letter itself. Better writing catches a reader's attention, holds it, and instills a memorable message. Keep this in mind when writing a sermon, too.

Let's look at a noncontroversial LTE to a local paper and see some examples of good, on-point openers that can jump out at an editor:

- I want to thank you for this morning's article about the interfaith food program and the description of how much work went into feeding so many people. As a member of the clergy, I appreciate learning of such activities. It was God's love in action.
- I brought my son to the hospital last week for an injured ankle and luckily nothing was broken. But I want to express my thanks for the warm and careful attention we received from all the emergency room staff. As a pastor, I visit folks at the hospital all the time. I was comforted to witness caring and compassionate health care, this time from the perspective of the parent of a patient.
- I'd like to compliment the volunteers who helped out at the museum gala. I was there and was glad to see the lovely article in the paper. As a community leader, I am proud this noteworthy event captured attention.

Now you've got an opening that can catch the editor's attention, especially an editor who, like many of us, is tired of hearing from angry people and wants to take a positive approach. A letter that thanks the paper or appreciates something in the community is refreshing. With all the angry religious rhetoric that fills the news, a word of thanks from a person of faith is noticed and appreciated.

Stay with One Issue

You want people to remember what you wrote. Sticking to a single topic helps readers focus. It's nice when you run into someone in the supermarket who says, "I saw your letter!" But you really want to hear, "I saw your letter on the senior center and I agree with you." You want them to come away from your letter with a reaction that is on your point.

Deal with Rejections

Don't get discouraged. I see too many people give up after one rejection. The reality is that a good proportion of all letters wind up in the trash. The papers get plenty of letters—more than they can use. But when several letters on the same topic arrive at a small paper in the course of a week, the editor might well think, "Gee, there must be something going on here. Let's send a reporter out to do a story." Your letter may not get in, but thanks to you, an issue close to your heart is more likely to get the attention it deserves. If there is an article published, you have another opportunity to write yet another letter.

Final Pointers

Keep it simple. Use brief sentences. And don't overstate. We'll talk more about letters when we explore controversial issues.

Op-eds That Drive Home the Point

Obviously, an op-ed essay or opinion piece is more involved than an LTE. If you are new to all this, you might want to hold off on opinion pieces until you get through the chapters in this book on message triangles and talking points. A good op-ed identifies an issue, presents three points like a good sermon, and hammers away. When it comes to clergy and content, our pastoral care experience is the gold standard for making an argument. When other religious leaders throw Bible-peppered rhetoric stretched to suit their arguments, our real-life experience of standing with people in times of need—immigrants, families confronted by teen pregnancy pointing to the need for better sex education—cuts through the talk and gets to the heart. Here are some ways to emphasize your point.

Check the Newspaper or Blog Website for Submission Requirements

Like your LTE, your op-ed has limits on length and timeliness. You will want to know the preferred method of submission. Generally op-eds go in the body of an e-mail or via a form on a web link—again, few places open attachments. Be sure to include contact information for verification or editing questions—these details are generally not published. You can find out if they respond to rejections or, if they don't, how long to wait until you know they are not interested.

Some places consider multiple submissions; others don't. If they will consider a multiple submission, let them know if you sent to anyone else. Just don't *threaten* to send it to others if you don't hear from them. Generally, I send things out sequentially and wait until I hear—or not. Multiple submissions make things too complicated.

Open with an Engaging Hook

Like the LTE, the successful opinion piece intrigues the reader right off the bat. See how some of the national columnists do it; they often open cleverly in a way to make you want to read on. By developing this habit—starting with an engaging pitch, not too ratcheted up—and bringing it to your preaching, you'll do better on the pulpit, too. Here are some sample opening lines:

- Many people are surprised that a religious leader would take the time to write about the library. But as I child, I spent plenty of time in my local library. As a community leader, I want to support education, reading, and literacy.
- It's not often that clergy come forward over a zoning issue, but many religious leaders—including those of us signing this essay—believe in maintaining the residential character of our neighborhoods.
- As a member of the clergy who devotes many hours to caring for the elderly in our community, I was distressed to learn about the proposed cuts to senior programs.

Keep Some Tension in Your Writing

As you move into the op-ed and start thinking about your closing, introduce some contrary information or note. The tone shift will kindle a new spark of curiosity. Here are some examples:

- I know that there are all kinds of opinions on this issue. Someone even said we ought to let the conversation die down.
- People express a variety of ideas about the matter, some with strong feelings attached.
- To be sure, many people disagree with me. One even said that those who look at things the way I do are entirely wrong. But, at the end of the day, I am holding my ground. Let me provide one more reason.

Reference Your Beginning at the End

A wise person once said, "When we get to the end, we always go back to the beginning." That's an important observation about life. It's also a great strategy for closing an opinion piece. It shows organization. It's a powerful way to close a sermon, too.

Write a Brief Pitch That Serves as a Cover Letter

The pitch introduces yourself and your issue, explains why the issue is important to the reader and why you are the best person to write about the topic. A good preface to your op-ed can make the difference between publication and the waste bin.

Reuse an Old Sermon

Enough said. Just reread it, recheck for typos, and make sure your citations are correct. Then send it in as your newly repurposed opinion piece.

Deal with Rejection

If you don't hear anything after their stated time, write it off or resubmit. If you decide to resubmit, send it in, call to make sure they got it, and ask if they might be interested in running it. Don't get angry. If you *are* angry, don't show it. They are as busy as we are. If they send you a rejection e-mail, respond with appreciation for the consideration. They didn't have to contact you and they might remember you next time. Then send the essay someplace else immediately. When I am in the midst of a writing burst, I can have several pieces circulating and get a blizzard of rejections—so many that I use a spreadsheet to keep track.

Accepting and Preparing for an Interview

When a reporter calls, don't you have to answer the questions on the spot? Everybody does that, right? That's what I used to think, but the reality is otherwise. Freedom of speech means the freedom not to speak, and nobody should judge you any the worse for turning a reporter down. You can decline without being quoted as having offered the dreaded "No comment!" Why is "No comment!" no good? Consider these examples:

- When asked about the allegations, he replied, "I have no comment."
- He responded, "I plead the Fifth" in an apparent effort to avoid self-incrimination.
- The rabbi said he has nothing to say about the religious symbol in the public park.

You get the idea. "No comment" says "I did something wrong" or "I have something to hide" or "I just don't care." Nevertheless, just because a reporter asks doesn't mean you have to respond right away, if at all.

I avoid interviews with reporters who are hostile to things I stand for, and I encourage you to reject those as well. Even if all my answers are appropriate, I expect to come out looking bad, no matter what. A series of full-length feature movies could be made composed of video clips of smart, skilled, and experienced people tripped up by smarter, better skilled, and more experienced hostile interviewers. Never be so desperate for coverage that you talk with someone from someplace you do not respect. Besides, their audience is pretty set in their ways and we are unlikely to change any minds—that's not my choir; it is someone else's. Of course, some people do rise above their interviewers, but don't count on it. *Reporters and interviewers want to make themselves look good—they are less concerned about me or you.*

If you are worried about being misrepresented by a reporter, go ahead and ask to read the entire article before it goes to press. The response will likely be "no." After all, I don't let my congregation review my sermons before I preach. Reporters will likely e-mail or read back a quote if you ask, but you have no control over how the quote is framed. All that being said, I know that some folks disagree and will take the interview no matter what. Good luck!

Consider informing someone where you work—a senior rabbi, senior minister, lay leader, or supervisor—before speaking with the press. They may have some important information about the topic or the reporter. What's more, they may not take kindly to finding you in the paper without knowing in advance. They will probably ask you to clarify whether you are speaking in a personal capacity or in the name of the organization. If you are talking about a program or holiday observance, go ahead and speak for your organization. If the interview is about anything controversial, speak in your own name and during the interview *underscore that you are speaking for yourself alone and not for your group.*

If you are inclined to take an interview—TV, radio, newspaper, magazine, blog—you also have the right to know a few things of your reporter. You get to ask the first questions:

- *Who do you work for?* I want to know that the publisher is reliable and accurate and will treat me fairly.
- *What issue are you covering?* I don't want to be asked about one issue when the story is about another.
- *What are you planning to say?* Tell me your angle.
- *What do you do at the newspaper?* Reporter, editor, or intern?
- *How do you see me fitting into your story?*
- *What will you need to know?* Do I need to get information from someone, or will I have to do any research? Do I have the time for all this?

- *How can I reach you?* I might think of something additional after the interview is over, or need to correct or clarify a point. I want to make sure that I am talking to the person I think I am talking to.
- *Who else are you interviewing?* Is it someone who is hostile to my position or to me personally? Will this influence how readers will consider my remarks?
- *Am I the focus or do you just want a brief comment?*
- *Do you need a photo?* This is a great opportunity to grab more attention.
- *When will the piece run?* I'd like to know when to look for it, and I want to tell others to look for it, too.

For broadcast interviews, you can also ask:

- *Will it be live or taped?* Taped is a lot less stressful, and you can ask them to edit out something you don't like.
- *Will the format be news, talk, feature, debate, panel, or call-in?* You can bring notes to a radio interview. You can provide written material for a press interview or even respond by e-mail. For a call-in, if you trust your host, you can also expect some help with a difficult call.

When and How to Decline an Interview

There are perfectly good reasons to decline an interview. I'll decline when I:

- Don't have the time to practice, prepare, research, or speak with others
- Don't know enough about the topic
- Can't present a clear, concise message
- Can't speak without getting angry or upset
- Am deferring to my senior rabbi who wants to be interviewed instead of me
- Don't want to be a reporter's piñata that is badgered with questions until I break and all the answers fall out of me like toys and treats at a birthday party

When declining, you don't have to explain yourself. Just be polite and credible, especially if you want the reporter to call you again in the future. You can say:

- I am not speaking with the press right now, but I appreciate your inquiry.
- I generally don't give interviews. Thank you for your interest, though.
- I am in the middle of doing something urgent, and I will not be able to comment by your deadline. I wish the situation were otherwise.
- I need clearance from my communications committee and my senior minister, and I will not be able to reach them by your deadline.
- I am not an expert in this area. Please call again when you are writing about something else.
- I have to meet several other deadlines.
- I am in the middle of several emergencies and need to focus my attention on them.

How to Buy Time

You can say:

- I will send you a written statement later.
- I will e-mail a statement by 5:00 p.m. today.

And if that doesn't work:

- I am sorry that I cannot pull my thoughts together by your deadline. Hopefully things will fit better next time.

Having a Successful Interview

We will get to message triangles and talking points later. Don't talk to the press until you know about these things. For now, keep in mind these tips:

- Responding by e-mail can be easier, less stressful, and less likely to lead to misquote.
- Get the reporter's deadline and give yourself time to research and think.
- Know your reporter. Watch the show, listen to the radio broadcast, or read other things the reporter has written.

2/19/18

- Realize that even sympathetic reporters ask "push" questions.
- Get to your point right away. Don't wait until the middle of the interview. You need to start at the outset. Make your point in every question. Take the initiative. Drive it home at the end of the interview. We will get to "points" in the next chapters.
- Keep responses clear, concise, and simple. Don't carry on.
- Talk in sound-bites—"ink bites" for print. Two or three sentences, tops.
- Pause between the question and answer to allow a few seconds for thinking.
- At the end of the interview, reiterate your main points. Say something like, "The most important thing to remember is ..." or "I hope your readers understand that...."
- If asked more than one question at a time, answer the one you like best. They'll re-ask about the others if they really want to know.
- You can mention your website or Facebook page.
- Don't fill in the silence; let the reporter do that. Filling the silence is a quick way to go off message. Say only what you prepared.

Nothing Is Off the Record

Assume the microphone is always on, even if the reporter turns it off. You don't want to be caught in a gaffe—saying what you really think when you didn't mean to say it. You never know when you will become a reporter's "anonymous source." I know that some disagree, but this is what I think:

- A newspaper reporter tapes the interview and turns off the recorder when it seems like the interview is over. Then the reporter asks about another issue. Your response is *on* the record.
- At a friendly lunch with a reporter, the conversation wanders to work and the people in the office. This conversation is *on* the record.
- A reporter asks, "Can I ask you, off the record?" Your response is *on* the record. You may find yourself quoted as "an unnamed source."
- Remember: Your friends are your friends, and reporters are reporters. Friends are friends because they keep confidences. Reporters are reporters because they report.

Handling Pastoral Questions

These situations all have something in common:

- A reporter asks about a family left bereft by an accident.
- The press wants to know what it was like to officiate at a wedding for a famous person.
- The media is interested in a recently jailed member of the congregation.

The truthful response is, "This is personal stuff and it's none of your business. I keep secrets. If you want to know about the family, call the family." But you really can't say that, as much as you may want to. Instead, you can say:

- We are a caring community and we stand by our members.
- We do not comment on specific pastoral issues.
- We respect people's privacy in our congregation.
- Our hearts go out to the family.

Confidentiality is a hallmark of clergy work. It speaks to the reason why people trust us with their life stories. It's also a good idea to avoid telling specific stories about people in sermons, the newspapers, and the like, no matter how well you can disguise the story. I know many clergy do this, but I would hate to hear about me from the pulpit or in the newspaper, even if I am the only one who knows that it is me. If you want to do this, get permission first. Consider saying that you have permission when you tell the story—you don't want to deter others from confiding in you.

Preparing for Broadcast Media

If offered the opportunity to do a pre-interview, grab it! You'll be more relaxed. Arrive early. Learn what you can by talking with the staff or the host. And remember, everything you say is on the record. Ask for a glass of water—you'll need it!

Sounding Good on Radio

Radio allows for bringing notes to expand on your remarks, especially for an extended conversation. If you are taking the interview from an office, control the background noises and distractions by turning off the computer and cell phone. Be sure to mute any phones. Make sure your voice is animated; some people are more natural than others. I have to pay attention or I'll sound disinterested. Call in on a landline instead of a cell. It's more reliable and sounds better.

Looking Good on TV

It's important to know how to sit, where to look, and how to move on camera. How you present yourself affects what people hear. Here are some tips on how to dress, posture, and presentation.

How to dress

- Wear plain, solid-color clothing. Avoid plaids, stripes, and busy designs.
- If offered makeup, wear it. Guys too.
- Keep hair away from the eyes.
- Wear something that identifies you as a religious person, such as a clergy collar, *kipah*, or other religious symbol.
- To prevent the collar of a blazer bunching up behind the neck, sit on the bottom hem.
- Keep jewelry simple; avoid things that make noise when moving. Avoid shiny jewelry that reflects camera lights.
- Men should shave right before to avoid the shadow.

Posture, movement, and presentation

- Sit straight, back in your chair, comfortably.
- If you are standing, hold your arms at your sides. Putting your hands behind the back throws the chest forward. Holding your hands in front of the body gets in the way. Keep one foot perpendicular to the other for balance and stability.
- Don't nod unless you want to show you agree.
- Smile somewhat but avoid the constant grin. Smile when introduced.

- Move around as little as possible. Don't sway, rock, fidget, or swivel around in a chair. Hand movements should be slow, minimal, and small.
- On camera, look where you are told and hold that focus. Wandering eyes leave a bad impression.

Avoiding trouble

- Watch the program beforehand; see how guests are treated, how the camera covers the guests, how the interviewer opens and closes, and what kind of "surprise" questions you might expect.
- Assume the microphone and cameras are always on. People in the studio are listening, and anything you say can come up in an interview.
- If you are on a panel and another panelist attacks you, don't get angry. Let your body language show you disagree. Shake your head as if to say "No." Taking notes during the attack, whether or not you plan to use them, looks like you are preparing a rebuttal—good idea.

Following Up

Once the interview comes out, you can send the reporter a note of appreciation if you like. If you spot an error, request a correction if you feel it is important enough. Don't get angry. Think about what you learned from the experience and what you will do next time— differently or the same.

2/25/18 ▬▬▬

Someone stole my snow powder paint at Atria + my unopened applegreen paint on the top shelf I don't think it was a resident it was too high up for them to retrieve easily

7

Raising the
Controversial Issues

2/25/18

As part 2 opened, we explored ways to speak about controversial issues like health care and immigration with dignity and respect. Additional suggestions include inviting others to stand with you and making it religious from the start.

First, when you get a press call about something noncontroversial, such as a congregational holiday celebration, an interfaith Thanksgiving service, or a community gathering, you can expect a warmer, more relaxed conversation, but it still pays to review the checklists and gather your thoughts. Be prepared to describe what makes you proud of your faith and what makes your congregation special. Take advantage of the opportunity. However, when the interview topic is controversial, you need to take extra steps to present a clear, concise, positive, and compelling message.

When it comes to controversy, you don't have to go it alone with a letter, newspaper interview, or TV appearance. You might feel more comfortable (and have greater impact) in the company of others from a variety of faith communities. Including others not only means you won't stick out so much but also demonstrates the breadth and depth of support for your position. You'll present a more compelling argument and leave a stronger impression. On issues such as abortion and stem cell research, religious opponents consist of only one or two groups, while many faiths stand in support. There is strength in that diversity. Some newspapers don't include all the signers of a group letter, limiting published signatures to just a couple. However, an editor may make an exception when told that religious diversity makes the letter work. Almost all the media samples in this book are first person; change the language as appropriate.

Making it religious from the start calls for more than an opening like: "We need to end this war." That's good, but it can be improved by giving it a voice of faith. Instead, begin with: *"As a member of the religious community*, I believe we need to end this war." The combination of capacity (religious) and issue (war and peace) adds to your voice. You bring faith to the public eye; you bring faith to life. Here are some other openers for various controversial issues:

- As a person of faith, I believe that stem cell research must move ahead. We honor God's gift of wisdom by searching for new ways to heal conditions like blindness, heart disease, and serious burns.
- As a lifelong Christian, I have an opinion about cervical cancer vaccination, one that differs from what many people expect to hear.
- As someone who goes to church regularly, I want to underscore the message of your editorial on terrorism. We have to stop equating violence with faith.
- As an adviser to our synagogue's youth group, I believe that teens need the medically accurate, age-appropriate information that sex education provides. Telling the truth is an important religious value.

Here are some other religious approaches on the environment, poverty, and education:

- As a pastor in the community, I draw from my faith teachings when it comes to caring about and for the environment.
- As a person of faith, I believe we need to do better when it comes to the poor.

- Many religious people are concerned about the quality of education in our communities. We value knowledge and support an investment in quality schools.

You can follow up with a personal detail or reflection on these issues:

- My family and I are avid hikers. We appreciate the natural beauty of our community as a sign of God's grace.
- I, along with members of our congregation, volunteer at the local soup kitchen.
- I never forget that I am a product of public education.

You might add a few facts, statistics, or information taken from an advocacy website, a gracious but firm conclusion, and your letter to the editor is done and on its way.

Use Emotion, but Don't Go Overboard

It's fine to express distress or concern, but watch the tone. Many letters in a local newspaper open with "I was angry" or "I was appalled." The harsh emotions distract from the argument; the feelings become the center of attention at the cost of the issue. Show upset, but use a measured voice. I'd rather be "distraught" or "concerned" than "outraged." Instead of opening with "That was the final straw," it's better to be "distressed." Measured words like "distress" or "concern" are also more intriguing: What's the writer thinking?

Take the High Road

Open with a positive voice, one that reflects positively on you and your community position. Express appreciation: "I was glad to read about the ambitious art program in the public schools." You now have an editor's attention. Then go on to say, "However, as a member of the clergy, I am concerned about pressuring students to include religious themes in their personal art work." Consider a letter thanking an elected leader for speaking up or for voting in a particular way. Officials and staff monitor the media. They use Google alerts to track media hits. Make sure that a letter like this speaks in a personal capacity and does not reference your congregation.

- The op-ed essay this weekend spoke to an important issue: minimum wage. As a pastor to families confronted by significant financial challenges, I can attest to the many hard-working but woefully underpaid individuals and heads of household who cannot make ends meet.
- It should not come as a surprise that a member of clergy like me would be concerned about voting rights. Unlike many quoted in the article last Tuesday, I believe we need to do what we can to ensure that every eligible voter in our community is able to vote.
- I am glad to see continuing coverage of the problem of affordable housing. As a rabbi who talks to many singles and families in the course of a week, I know how big an issue this is. As surely as we seek God's shelter, we seek a place to live without worry.

Make Your Own Arguments

I used to think I had to show I understood my detractors. I'd cite their arguments and then dispute them, as if to say, "See how smart I am! I am smarter than they are!" But with word limits at the newspaper (and patience limits in the sanctuary), I make better use of time *by making my good points*; I avoid wasting time by rehashing someone else's bad ones. Don't repeat the point you object to. If you have to, refer to it broadly without using that language. Then go right to your argument. For example:

- We hear plenty about school budget cuts and class size. As a parent and community leader, I want to describe the hardship these proposed cuts would impose.
- I know that people disagree with me about gun control. But I want everyone to know that my religious group has taken a clear and unequivocal position on this important issue, underscoring the need to provide safe streets for our children.
- Plenty has been said about homelessness and poverty. I'd like us to talk about what my faith says and what God calls us to do.

Speak in a Personal Voice

Talk about your life experience. It adds clarity to your argument and warmth to your voice and demonstrates your personal stake. Opponents can cite statistics or throw their experience around, but what you know, do, and feel is yours, so state your personal case and hold your ground.

- As a parent and religious leader, I want all the children in our community to have safe and caring homes, just as God loves all children. That is why I support the proposed youth center and the positive influence it will have on home lives in our neighborhoods.
- As a lifelong member of the community, I think it's best that the public park be neutral toward religion during holiday seasons. City hall must not favor one faith over another.
- As an army veteran, I have some strong feelings about war and peace, and my faith takes some clear positions as well.
- When I went to school, I got the science in the classroom and the faith at home and at my church. That's a great way for our children to learn about God's creation.

Focus on Policy, Not Politics

It took me a long and painful time to learn that it's not about politics—who holds office or their political party. It's not about terms like "liberal" and "conservative," "Democrat" and "Republican," or "religious right" and "social justice." There is very little need to mention elected leaders by name. Parties, philosophies, and people are red flags; the audience responds viscerally and forgets about the issue—"Oh, the president is too this!" or "The mayor is too that!" or "What do you expect from a Republican?" and "Let me tell you about the religious right!" This rhetoric and thinking makes for a bad distraction. Keep the argument about faith and what that faith has to say on the topic; avoid politicians and politics. When someone drags you there, bring them back. Here are some ideas:

- People who attack the mayor over school safety are missing the point. We need to turn our focus from her to the importance of making sure our children and their teachers are safe and secure.
- I can tell you that when it comes to freedom of speech, it's not Democrat versus Republican by any means. People of all political parties have strong opinions on all sides of this issue.
- I know that many folks blame the president for the ongoing overseas military involvement. Let's look at the bigger picture and see what we can do to end the conflict.

Reach Out and Use Their Language and Images

"Liberals" get miscast as supporters of big government who are soft on national security and hostile to big business. We get mischaracterized as the kind of people who would let the "stubborn and rebellious child" go free—and reward him, too! Don't let them do this to you. You stand for justice, moderated by compassion. You want to hold folks accountable for their wrongdoings and at the same time work toward a better tomorrow. It's important to use language that accurately reflects the full spectrum of your beliefs. It is equally important to stand up and speak out when your beliefs are disparaged.

Talking about immigration? Then call for policies that support national security, safeguard our borders, and provide a realistic, workable plan to address the situation. Concerned about overemphasis on the threat of terrorism? Affirm your loyalty to our country. Cite your military service or that of loved ones and friends. Talk about your invocation at the Veteran's Day parade; describe your admiration for those who devote themselves to the security of the nation. Speak about your love for country, its history and founders, and how happy you are to live in the United States. The "borrowed language" is italicized:

- We can *establish a good economy* that protects God's creation.
- When women and families have access to reproductive health care, including contraception and abortion care, they have children when the time is right for them and *build stronger families and lives*.

- I want schools that provide *structure* and teach *self-discipline.*
- Making sure that kids have proper medical attention keeps them healthier and builds a foundation for having *a successful and productive life.*
- Public assistance programs enable families to become better at *helping themselves and to contribute to the greater good.*
- My faith has long supported the value of knowledge, and I want our *tax dollars invested* in quality public education.
- Expanding the protections and responsibilities of marriage to same-gender couples *strengthens the moral fabric of the community.*
- As a member of the Jewish faith, I want to point out the persecution our people have suffered in other lands. *I am grateful to live here with my family. And I want this country and this world to become a better place for all children of God*, those born here and those who recently arrived.
- *I was proud to participate in the Memorial Day parade* and appreciate the special role that clergy had to play in the commemoration.

Demonstrate Interfaith Cooperation

People expect religious folk to be angry, especially at each other, so we can get their attention when we agree across religious lines. Talk about interfaith cooperation and cut through the bias. Try submitting a letter like one of these, from time to time:

- I speak with people from churches, synagogues, and mosques all the time. We sponsor a wonderful community education forum and invite you to join us.
- That was a great article about the community Thanksgiving service. It was thrilling to see people of our varied faiths gather in prayer. The service and article remind us all about the blessings of being Americans.
- I sit on the municipal senior and aging commission, joining with religious leaders from a spectrum of faiths in support of the betterment of our community and honoring our elders. That's why I appreciate the article last week.

Don't Get Upset when Letter Writers Criticize You or Disagree

Expect your letter to provoke comments, both supportive and critical. You will not have the final word, and I generally don't bother to write a letter of rebuttal. Assume that you will be questioned, and take heart that you went on record; people will remember what you said. Arousing opposition demonstrates effectiveness.

8

Building and Using a Message Triangle

It was the morning after Election Day. The intercom buzzed. There was a call from a reporter. One of our members had run for office and lost. What did people at the temple think? Granted, there was no real problem speaking with the press. The election was over and I couldn't possibly be using my position to influence a campaign just ended. But I still hesitated—it was all about appearance. A public statement regarding an election, at any point in time, could be viewed as partisan. And truth was no one at the temple said anything to me about the race, and I certainly didn't want to say *that*. After all, could you imagine reading, "The way the rabbi spoke, no one at the temple seemed to care"? I could have tried to wiggle out of the interview: "I'm busy. Try me later." I could hope the reporter would move on to someone else. But I took the call and said just this: "We are a caring temple community. We stand with our members through ups and downs."

"Just one more question, Rabbi. What do you hear about the rabbi over at the Orthodox synagogue? I hear he's caught in a contract dispute." There were rumors he had taken another job, left by mutual agreement, or had been let go. But I don't like to repeat rumors, not around the community and certainly not to the media. The proper response would have been "No comment." So I imagined reading,

"When asked about the situation in the other congregation, Rabbi Ross refused to comment," as if I was trying to hide something, which I was. What's more, I had spoken with that rabbi at one point, but I wasn't going to say that to the press either. There is no obligation to respond to every question a reporter asks or even to agree to be interviewed to begin with.

I said, "I don't have any information to share." Now that was the truth and it never made it to print, as I expected. But the reporter didn't give up. "Your colleagues are talking. Can you say something off the record?" Again, I said, "I have no information to share." And that was that.

Crafting Your Message and Staying on It

It's not easy or simple to do a media interview. With as many interviews as I have done, I still prepare for each one very carefully. Let's take a moment to reflect on that call. When it comes to talking with a reporter, remember these tips:

- Make your point and drive it home.
- Don't go off your point.
- Repeat your point until he or she gets it.

As for making my "point" in that interview, just what was it? "We are a caring temple community. We stand with our members through ups and downs." That was it, a pastoral perspective. "We are a caring temple community." Here I had a reporter who would, at the most, include a brief clip from me. I was not the focus of the story—the candidate was the focus in one, and that rabbi was the focus in the other. I knew any references to me would be secondary. So I took the opportunity to present my congregation in a positive and attractive light. That was my goal for this interview. I wanted my reader to come away saying, "Isn't it great to be part of a spiritual community where people stand together through all the challenges of life?"

Staying on point does not come easily or naturally. It goes against just about everything I learned in seminary, where, when it came to pastoral counseling, they taught me to *listen with all three ears*. After all, a compassionate pastor hears, reflects, and responds, just as the counselee asks and needs. But we don't do that with a reporter, even one who is friendly or sympathetic. Taking an interview requires preparation—knowing what to say, how to say it, how to stay on the message, and how to get back to the message when it looks like the interview is getting away from you. When it comes to media, *I barely listen with one ear*. Instead, I think of what I am there to say; I stay on my point and drive it home. Building a media tool known as a message triangle is a great first step.

When it came to a controversial issue in my earlier years, say a sermon or an interview on a hot topic, I assumed I needed to give a thorough answer. I'd cite as many religious authorities as possible because I wanted the people to know their religious heritage and to respect my authority. I also believed in turning to the social, political, and cultural sources to support me in a way that showed "See how smart I am!" But this display of wisdom only earned groans that said, "Oh, no! There he goes again!" I met more success with the message triangle.

Like any triangle, a message triangle has three corners. The corners speak:

- Concisely
- Passionately
- Memorably

The corners rely on:

- Inarguable fact
- Logical development
- Related conclusions

The triangle corners build by:

- Citing a problem
- Suggesting a solution
- Explaining why that solution is best

The triangle resolves controversy by presenting:

- A statement of fact
- A challenge to that statement
- A response

Triangles work well for religious leaders when they:

- Speak emotionally rather than intellectually
- Save details—science, statistics, and stories—for talking points
- Talk about faith

Don't say anything that is not in the triangle; don't get drawn off your message. No matter what the reporter asks or your congregant says, bring the conversation back to your point.

- Don't add.
- Don't embellish.
- Don't stray.

The three corners of the triangle, and the talking points we will discuss in the next chapter, are all that I have to say to a reporter. Going off the triangle is the easiest way to lose. The center of the triangle has a core message that can be summed up in a few words. In the next chapter, we will focus on messages related to our earlier themes: the widow (the woman), the stranger (the immigrant), and the orphan (the youth). For now, a core message is something like this:

- Reproductive rights: "Women and families need to be able to get quality and affordable care."
- Immigration: "Immigrants are children of God, just like us."
- The needs of youth: "Investing in children and their education builds our communities and America."

Your core message is the reason why you are talking with the press, what you want them to carry away. If it takes more than a sentence to state your core message, split it up, hold onto the point you need, and put the rest of the language away to use for your triangle corners and talking points. Once you have that core message, make up a list of why that message is important, working your way up to a total of six to ten reasons. The list includes evidence, supporting statements, historical facts, personal experience, or a pastoral care story. Focus on ideas and language that convey emotions and drive action. Then pick the three most significant points, the ones that most resonate with your core message and will stir your audience. Those go onto the corners of your triangle. In the next chapter we will also see how to use the put-aside points as talking points.

Three main points are ideal for structuring an op-ed, an interview, or a sermon. More than three points overwhelms your reporter and your audience; they might also be difficult for you to remember during an interview. Fewer than three points leaves a message sounding narrow and without depth. And always, during an interview—or under a grilling by a difficult congregant during a social hour—stay on the triangle. Later on we will talk about bridge language to get you back on your points. First, let's build up a triangle, with the core in the middle.

It may feel odd or unnatural to communicate with triangles and talking points. But Bible people communicated the same way. In the book of Exodus (chapter 10), Moses and Aaron demand that Pharaoh free the people of Israel. Who could forget their core message? *Let my people go!*

We have a special
relationship with God.

**Let my
people go!**

Obey or face
terrible consequences.

God wants the
people free.

Check out the story and see how they build their triangle. That core rests on the biblical covenant, point one: *We have a special relationship with God.* The covenant demands honoring God's plan, which is point two: *God wants the people free.* And a failure to follow God's plan will bring ten plagues, point three: *If you disobey, you will face terrible consequences.* Again, the rest is history: *Let my people go!*

In another example, dream interpretation was a respected profession in the days of the Hebrew Bible, as seen in the story of an earlier King Pharaoh distraught over puzzling dreams of corn ears and cattle (Genesis 41). The king frantically canvassed the royal dream interpreters for an explanation meeting his satisfaction, to no avail. Then the royal cup bearer recalled the highly accurate dream-reading skills of Joseph, who was wrongly imprisoned for a crime he did not commit. The king released Joseph and brought him to court, where he provided an interpretation that fit this triangle:

Joseph's core message was: *God has given me a gift.* The first corner of the triangle offered a simple explanation of the dreams: *Seven years of abundant harvest will be followed by seven years of famine.* The second corner pointed to what had to be done: *If Egypt stores food during the years of plenty, there will be ample supply for the years of famine.* And the third corner says that Pharaoh needs to put someone smart in charge of this major public works project: *You know who.* Joseph got the job and saved the nation.

Abundance will be followed by famine.

God has given me a gift.

Prepare for tough times.

Make Joseph responsible.

In another triangle, in Genesis 28, Jacob—frightened by the wrath of his brother, Esau—fled for his life on foot. In the dark of night, tired and alone in the wilderness, Jacob rested his head on an impromptu pillow of a rock. He endured restless sleep featuring a dramatic dream of angels ascending and descending a ladder spanning the earth and the heavens, and God's reassuring promise of blessing and safety.

Jacob's core message is: *God is with me and with our people.* The triangle shows how God chooses certain times and places for holiness: *This place is awesome!* God comes unexpectedly: *God is here and I had no idea!* Loyalty to God brings rewards and obligates thanksgiving: *If God is with me and protects me on this journey and gives me food to eat and clothing to wear, and I return safely to my father's home, then the Eternal will be my God and this stone, which I set up as a marker, will be God's home, and I will tithe to You all that You gave me.*

Let's use the triangle to communicate at the church. Say you're having dinner with a member, and you know that he or she has invited an unaffiliated friend, a disciple of Sigmund Freud, someone who thinks that religion is a figment of the mind and of no use to a rational person. In contrast, you believe that religion plays a positive role in life. You know the topic will come up—it always does. While you want to make your point—after all, you're the pastor, so you have to say something—you don't want to get angry. So turn to the creation story, build a message triangle, and stay on point with a core message of: *I affirm faith.*

These are the corners:

- Religion was a good influence from the start: *In the beginning …*
- Religion contributes to a better world: *God called it very good.*
- Religion is a positive force in my personal, familial, and communal life.

My money says this person will back off.

In another example, let's say you're going to brunch with a different member, this one with a disciple of Karl Marx as a friend. Marx thinks that religion is a crutch for the weak and the Bible is nothing more than a ploy of the wealthy used to exploit the poor. In contrast, you believe that the Hebrew Bible teaches a critical moral lesson when instructing us to help those in need. So you build a triangle with a core message of: *I affirm faith.*

These are the corners:

- People are echoes of the Divine: *Male and female are created in God's image.*
- What we say to those who exploit people: *Let my people go!*
- What to do when people are made into underdogs: *Love the widow, the stranger, and the orphan.*

Again, you may not win the argument, but you can win the peace. Let's turn to some other issues—stem cell research and the size of government—for more triangle examples.

Stem Cell Research

Stem cell research brings hope of healing for juvenile type 1 diabetes, serious burns, spinal cord injuries, Parkinson's disease, and other life-threatening and life-altering medical conditions. Human embryonic stem cell research, the most promising kind, upsets abortion opponents for relying on stem cells taken from human embryos, destroying the embryo in the process. Despite their religious objections and attempts to ban embryonic stem cell research, many religious leaders believe that it is the right thing to do. This research relies on embryos left over from in vitro fertilization. Too many were made, and those remaining will never be used to establish a pregnancy. The embryos sit in frozen storage, where they will eventually deteriorate or be discarded. Only a very small percentage will be given to others for having children—there are just too many; they have no future. So it makes perfect sense to turn to these embryos to try to help people in need. After all, attempting to save a life has a morally higher calling than trying to preserve something that will be destroyed or deteriorate anyway. Here's a stem cell message triangle:

Start with a core statement, a statement of faith you can't dispute: *Doctors, nurses, and researchers are God's agents of healing and comfort.* Then build your triangle, something else you can't dispute: *We all agree on the importance of bringing healing and comfort to the injured and sick.* Add another thing you can't dispute: *Stem cell research enjoys support from many religious groups—Christian, Jewish, and Muslim.* End with a conclusion growing from the indisputable points: *The moral high ground has us turning to stem cell research, bringing hope to people confronted by life-threatening and life-altering medical conditions, including juvenile type 1 diabetes, serious burns, spinal cord injuries, Parkinson's disease, and much more. I hope stem cell research cures my cousin's illness.* There we are. Stress the indisputable: religious people agree. Highlight the emotional: bringing healing to the sick. Make the argument religious, and make the argument personal.

Size of Government

The debate over the size of government gets bundled with arguments about social programs that purportedly don't work, schools that allegedly don't teach, and so on. As President Ronald Reagan said, "I'm here to tell you today, and I hope Congress takes notice, what ails us now is what has always ailed us: the Federal Government is too big, and it spends too much money."[1] "Big government" critics harp on government failures or inefficiencies. They single out a handful of "cheats" who supposedly "game the system." They use these rare examples as a rhetorical justification for shutting down programs that provide essential services to so many others who are deserving and in need. This sounds like the old religious argument that maintains, "I worked hard for my money. My wealth is a sign of God's blessing. It would be wrong to give it to someone who didn't earn it." They run for office on the theme that the best government is one that cuts jobs, even as they seek government jobs for themselves. But let's get back to the message.

A standard response is "I am opposed to war, and I have to pay for it! So, if you're opposed to paying for schools, you should have to pay for them, too." It's a good argument, but it doesn't win the day. Let's look at a message triangle, with the talking points added. The core message: *Only the government can provide a safety net.* Next, move off their argument to yours by starting with a statement of fact: *The size of government is not the issue.* Finally, suggest a solution: *We need to support government when it performs essential services*:

- Don't you want the fire department to come to your home when there is a need? Who is supposed to pay for that?
- When you get on a plane, don't you want the government to make sure the tires are good and the oil has been changed?
- When your kid bites into a slice of pizza, don't you want to know that someone inspected the cheese? The food industry can't police itself.
- If I think that the kids next door are being abused, who am I supposed to call?
- Don't you want clean water when you turn on the faucet?
- Who will make sure that the bridge you drive over to get to work won't collapse?
- We need to provide a strong military.
- It's not the size of government, but what it does.
- Let's start by identifying essential programs.

You'll want to anticipate criticism: *I know that there are some people who game the system.*

- Why deprive *everyone* because of a few bad apples?
- The important thing is taking care of people who deserve our support.
- I'm more interested in protecting those who deserve the protection.
- You can't let an egregious exception be an excuse for ignoring a big problem.
- The "moral hazard" argument doesn't sway me. Sorry.

Appeal to the emotions: government protects kids in need. Appeal to the personal: protect your property from harm, give you a road to drive on. And speak in a positive voice. The next chapter builds message triangles on our core message—the widow, the stranger, and the orphan—and fills them out with talking points.

Building on the Triangle

The Platform of Faith

When a nationally recognized religious opponent of abortion came to town to protest, a television reporter called the women's health center for a response. "This is a religious dispute," said the health center director. "You need to talk to a religious person. I have a minister you might try. She is well acquainted with the issues and is comfortable talking with the media. Let me get in touch with her and see if she is available." The director called the minister to give her a heads-up. The minister took the call from the reporter and agreed to give the interview later that day. She then alerted the church moderator, who offered support. The minister took a breath and, knowing that you don't have to make it all up yourself, turned to her files, went online for more info, compiled talking points, and built them into a triangle.

- First she wrote in the middle: *Many clergy stand with the women and their doctors and nurses.*
- For one corner, she wrote: *Different faiths have different teachings about our intimacy.*
- For another, she put: *The health center is a vital community resource.*

- And for the last corner: *My experience as a pastor demonstrates that when it comes to health care, it is best to let the woman make the decision.*

```
┌─────────────────────────────────────────────────┐
│              Different faiths have               │
│              different teachings.                │
│                                                  │
│                      ▲                           │
│                                                  │
│                   Clergy                         │
│                 stand with                       │
│                   women.                         │
│                                                  │
│      The health center is      The patient will make │
│        a vital resource.        a wise decision.     │
└─────────────────────────────────────────────────┘
```

The minister planned to describe the health center as a place that meets an essential local need. She pointed to the diversity of religious teaching on the issues. She underscored the tremendous religious support for women. And, if she had the opportunity during the interview, she would place priority on her work as a pastor and the lessons learned from that counseling experience. The minister had no interest or intention of rebutting—or even directly mentioning—the opposition. She made a note to herself to make sure to say that she was speaking *in her name only* and not for any group or organization.

Then she took those triangle points and added details—the talking points—to flesh out the arguments:

Many clergy stand with the women and their doctors and nurses:
- Groups opposed to abortion do not speak for me or for clergy from a wide spectrum of denominations, including Baptist, Episcopal, Methodist, Lutheran, Presbyterian, Unitarian, and others, as well as for rabbis and leaders of Islam.
- Our faiths teach that doctors and nurses are God's agents of comfort and healing.

- Doctors and nurses everywhere show God's love by caring for people in need.
- From the earliest days of the family-planning movement, clergy have come forward on behalf of women's health centers like this one.

She described the diversity of religious attitudes on the topic:

Different faiths have different teachings about our intimacy:
- People need to remember that there is more than one religious way to look at our intimacy.
- I believe that religious leaders who are against abortion should be prohibited from imposing their restrictions on folks who follow other faith teachings.
- As a life-loving faith community, we want families to have children when they decide it is right for them.
- It's not for the government to play favorites among religions or to referee a purely religious dispute like this one.
- As a member of the United Church of Christ, I am proud to say that our denomination has been a leader among churches on issues of justice related to women.

The minister spoke about meeting the medical needs in the neighborhoods:

The health center is a vital community resource:
- Ninety percent of what our health center does has nothing to do with abortion. Its services include life-saving annual checkups and cancer screenings.
- I don't know where people would turn for health care if the health center were to suddenly disappear.
- As a member of the clergy and a community leader, I appreciate having this community-based women's health center in our neighborhood.
- I am proud to say that I refer women and families I counsel to the health center for care.
- I have gone to the health center for my own medical needs.
- Doctors and nurses are God's agents of comfort and healing. They demonstrate God's love by caring for people in need.

Finally, and most critically, she pointed to her pastoral care experience:

My experience as a pastor demonstrates that when it comes to health care, it is best to let the woman make the decision:

- I have witnessed that ultimately this is her decision alone, between her and her God.
- When a woman knows her pregnancy is not right for her, she will do what she needs to do to make things right. That's why she has to be able to get safe, quality, and affordable medical care.
- When it comes to a health-care decision, including contraception and abortion care, my work as a pastor demonstrates that we need to let people make up their own minds about what they need to do and where to go for their medical care.
- The Hebrew Bible teaches us that Adam and Eve have the ability to make God-like decisions. People need to make up their own minds.
- Those seeking medical care need our support. They don't need uninvited legislators, judges, or religious leaders meddling in their private lives.

By all measures, when I saw this on TV, it worked.

Expanding Your Message Triangle with Talking Points

This section shows how to add talking points to the message triangle. "Talking points" have a bad reputation, implying that the person using talking points is a mouthpiece for a political agenda, just repeating what someone else told them to say. But talking points get plenty of use—not only because they work but because they are often true. Just because an idea comes up in a talking point doesn't make it bad. Talking points include all kinds of supportive information: statistics, academic studies, personal experience, denominational statements, professional opinions, and more. These details help flesh out the argument and make it more compelling.

Clergy talking points rely on the moral authority of faith and religious leadership, all taken from "the Platform of Faith." This includes the following:

- The experience of a pastor and the caring community.
- Disassociation—"Don't lump me with them."
- Nationally endorsed denominational statements and faith teachings.
- The perspective of a community leader.
- The personal voice: "I speak as a parent, husband, son, pastor, and more."
- Advocacy history: "Voices of faith have spoken about this for years."
- The patriotic argument.

Let's look back on the previous example to see how talking points drawn from the clergy platform fill out the triangle.

The experience of a pastor and the caring community:
- *Triangle corner:* My experience as a pastor demonstrates that when it comes to health care, it is best to let the woman to make the decision.
- *Talking point:* When a woman knows her pregnancy is not right for her, she will do what she needs to do to make things right. That's why she has to be able to get safe, quality, and affordable medical care. 3/2/18

Disassociation—"Don't lump me with them":
- *Triangle corner:* Different faiths have different teachings about our intimacy.
- *Talking point:* As a member of the United Church of Christ, I am proud to say that our denomination has been a leader among churches on issues of justice related to women.

Nationally endorsed denominational statements and faith teachings:
- *Triangle corner:* Many clergy stand with the women and their doctors and nurses.
- *Talking point:* Groups opposed to abortion do not speak for me or for clergy from a wide spectrum of denominations, including Baptist, Episcopal, Methodist, Lutheran, Presbyterian, Unitarian Universalist, and others, as well as for rabbis and leaders of Islam.

You can find specific denominational statements on moral agency and abortion at the close of chapter 3.

The perspective of a community leader:
- *Triangle corner:* The health center is a vital community resource.
- *Talking point:* Doctors and nurses are God's agents of comfort and healing. They demonstrate God's love by caring for people in need.

The personal voice: "I speak as a parent, husband, son, pastor, and more":
- *Triangle corner:* The health center is a vital community resource.
- *Talking point:* I have loved ones who have gone to the health center for their own medical needs.

Advocacy history: "Voices of faith have spoken about this for years":
- *Triangle corner:* Many clergy stand with the women and their doctors and nurses.
- *Talking point:* From the earliest days of the family-planning movement, clergy have come forward on behalf of women's health centers like this one.

Let's explore the Platform of Faith more deeply, starting with the perspective of a pastor and the caring community.

The Experience of a Pastor and the Caring Community

Religious leaders bring a unique perspective to the issue of reproductive health care. Clergy have real-life experience counseling women and families making medical decisions, giving them a special point of view and the ability to make a critical contribution to the debate. In social work school, I heard time and time again that "your advocacy is informed by your clinical experience." This means what we learn from working with people teaches us what to say to the media and to the folks who write the laws. This is especially true for the clergy and members of caring religious communities.

Any state capitol and legislative office building fills with people holding all sorts of opinions, including religious people who wave their Bibles in the air and cast aspersion on those who obtain or provide abortion care. They present "facts" directed to the intellect. We tell stories that open the heart. A supportive and positive religious voice relies, first of all, on the experience of being with people in prayer and in support when confronted by real-life challenges. Religious leaders come to the capitol and retell those stories, describe the lessons of "being present," with words and reflections—all this makes for compelling advocacy. The conclusions gleaned from pastoral care cut through the strident, negative rhetoric to convey a different and essential message about the needs of the woman and her family. Life experience is a sacred possession and stands as a moral calling into advocacy.

Many clergy are particularly comfortable talking about health care. Clergy and chaplains are a constant presence in medical facilities—nursing homes, hospitals, assisted living centers, and so on. Clergy are used to basic medical terminology and are acquainted with how people make medical decisions; hospital chaplains, in particular, have specialized training and experience. All this helps in advocacy. Of course, clergy obviously need to honor the role of the pastor as trusted confidant. It is never appropriate to share a story that allows anyone to be recognized.

Disassociation: "Don't Lump Me with Them"

Open your letter, opinion piece, or statement with a refreshing perspective. First, identify yourself as a person of faith, and your readers will likely and immediately think of the people they hear from all the time. Then distance yourself from the angry voices that get so much attention. Try something along these lines:

- While the article cited one religious leader with one religious opinion, I'd like to point out that this nation is blessed with a diverse array of teachings on many issues.
- Many people assume all clergy see something wrong with gay rights, just as the ones cited in the opinion piece last Wednesday. But, as a religious leader, I want to remind people about the wide spectrum of religious attitude on this very question.

- We have been hearing all too much from clergy who call global warming a myth, just as I read about this morning. As a rabbi, however, I must say that, along with my denomination and many others, I stand with the overwhelming consensus of scientific evidence. I believe global warming is real, it is caused by human activity, and we need to do something about it—fast!
- I'd like to remind everybody that there's a broad diversity of belief filling our houses of worship. No single faith or religious spokesperson enjoys a monopoly of opinion. It is time for another perspective for a change.

Disassociating yourself from the noise opens many doors to the media and government. You have a different viewpoint that stirs interest. Can't you hear them saying, "What? I thought all religious people oppose evolution! You mean, I was wrong?" Disabuse the mistaken impression that religion is a monolith and harbors only one authentic opinion. When an article or opinion piece presents just one religious voice and ignores the others, instead of getting angry and turning the page, take advantage of an opening to write a letter that says, "I appreciate the coverage of an important issue, but let's also hear a different point of view."

Nationally Endorsed Denominational Statements and Faith Teachings

Many religious groups endorse policy positions consistent with their faith teachings. The statements cover a wide range of topics, including women's health, immigration and children, moral agency, and church-state separation. Statements may cite biblical and later religious teachings, scientific and social science evidence, and more on behalf of their positions. The statements are products of a deliberative democratic process that includes clergy and/or lay leaders and are ratified by national church and synagogue bodies representing millions. Of course, no faith is a monolith; every denomination includes some who are not on board. Nevertheless, these statements represent the religious support of a denominational body.

Endorsements of access to reproductive health care—including contraception, sex education, and abortion care—can be found on the following denominational, interdenominational, and organizational websites:

- American Baptist Churches (www.ABC-USA.org)
- Catholics for Choice (www.CatholicsforChoice.org)
- Disciples of Christ (www.Disciples.org)
- Episcopal Church (www.EpiscopalChurch.org)
- Evangelical Lutheran Church in America (www.ELCA.org)
- Jewish Reconstructionist Federation (www.JRF.org)
- National Council of Jewish Women (www.ncjw.org)
- Presbyterian Church (USA) (www.PCUSA.org)
- Religious Coalition for Reproductive Choice (www.RCRC.org)
- Religious Disciples of Christ (www.disciples.org)
- Religious Institute (www.ReligiousInstitute.org)
- Union for Reform Judaism (www.URJ.org)
- Unitarian Universalist Association (www.UUA.org)
- United Church of Christ (www.UCC.org)
- United Methodist Church (www.UMC.org)
- United Synagogue for Conservative Judaism (www.USCJ.org)
- Women of Reform Judaism (www.WRJ.org)

Accurate talking points rely on current information about science, status of legislation, policy statements, statistics, and other points. Information is constantly changing. For the latest on reproductive rights, visit the following websites:

- Center for Reproductive Rights (www.ReproductiveRights.org)
- Guttmacher Institute (www.Guttmacher.org)
- NARAL Pro-Choice America (www.naral.org)
- Planned Parenthood Federation of America (www.PlannedParenthood.org)

The Perspective of a Community Leader

The vitality of a house of worship depends on the vitality of the larger community—the economy, its health care, cultural institutions, schools, and other aspects. Religious leaders and religious organizations have a stake in the well-being of our neighborhoods, a personal and organizational investment. This "skin in the game," as they say, serves as a source of knowledge and authority. People of faith can effectively address the media and policy makers as community leaders.

The Personal Voice:
"I Speak as a Parent, Husband, Son, Pastor, and More"

Religious leaders also speak in a personal, more intimate voice through a measured reference to personal life. Reminding the audience of our families, retirement concerns, medical needs, and paying our tax bills speaks to a commitment to the common good.

Advocacy History:
"Voices of Faith Have Spoken about This for Years"

Many denominations have a proud advocacy history, with some traditions going all the way back to Bible times. Citing that long-standing commitment lends a measure of strength to an argument; there is nothing new about religious leaders coming forward. It also responds to criticism from those who think religion must remain confined to the insides of a church or temple.

The Patriotic Argument

All too often, people dismiss other arguments by labeling them as "unpatriotic." Whenever possible, express your loyalty—emphasize support of the community, the economy, and the national well-being.

Having covered a woman's health and moral agency, now let's turn to additional message opportunities: immigration, children, and some thoughts on church-state separation.

The Immigration Message Triangle

The deeply rooted biblical teaching to love and care for the stranger speaks directly to the immigration debate. The blanket reference to "illegal immigration" is not only inaccurate; it's an unfair mischaracterization of the many immigrants in the United States within the law and contributing to the common good. It's helpful to draw from a broad range of concepts and language when dispelling mischaracterizations and distortions, including *language from all sides of the issue.* It appeals to a wider circle and makes an argument more compelling. Just tell the truth—it works!

Immigration opponents often present the issue as a simple problem with a simple solution, albeit a problem addressed in anger. The center of that triangle might look like this: *Immigrants deserve less than others.*

- Immigrants are here illegally.
- Immigrants don't contribute.
- Immigrants take advantage.

Let's start with that negative language to build our positive triangle. Counter "Immigrants deserve less than others" with a center that says: *Immigrants are children of God just like us.* Turn to the facts. "Immigrants are here illegally" becomes *The majority of immigrants are here legally and follow the law.* "Immigrants don't contribute" becomes *Many immigrants contribute more than they take, benefiting our nation and our communities.* And "Immigrants take advantage" becomes *Many immigrants do the right thing.*

Immigrants
honor the law.

**Immigrants
are children
of God.**

Immigrants contribute
more than they take.

Immigrants
do the right thing.

As the advocacy groups document, it's all true. Let's see how our triangle turns to the Platform of Faith to build talking points.

Immigrants are children of God just like us:
- *Faith teaching:* God loves each one of us, no matter when and where we were born.
- *Patriotic:* We have the brainpower to develop a smart, sensible, and ethical plan for immigration that recognizes our common humanity.
- *Patriotic:* We can develop policies that protect national security, safeguard public safety, protect and provide for the workforce, and treat all children of God fairly.
- *Faith teaching:* We were all immigrants in the days of Moses, desert wanderers, just as the Hebrew Bible says. Let's recall that spiritual heritage as we figure out how to treat immigrants today.

Many immigrants contribute more than they take, benefiting our nation and our communities:
- *Personal:* I was surprised to learn how many immigrants serve in our military. Where would our national security be without them?
- *Patriotic:* Many immigrants pay more in taxes than they will ever receive in benefits.
- *Community:* Last time you went to a neighborhood restaurant, your meal may well have been prepared by an immigrant.
- *Pastoral:* When I pay pastoral visits to the infirm, I witness how often immigrants provide caring personal attention.
- *Patriotic:* Immigrants pay sales tax on purchases and payroll tax at work.
- *Pastoral:* I know of many immigrants in our community who provide excellent care for the elderly.
- *Personal:* I'll bet that an immigrant handpicked that apple you just ate.

The majority of immigrants are here legally and follow the law:
- *Personal:* As any baseball fan knows, many immigrants play for our professional teams. It's all perfectly legal, and no one seems to complain.

- *Patriotic:* It's not feasible to throw them all out. There are probably more than ten million undocumented immigrants in the United States. Deporting a million a year—three thousand each day—would take ten years. We don't have the wherewithal to do that. Besides, let's recognize how many are here within the law.

Many immigrants do the right thing:
- *Advocacy history:* Our Jewish community took the lead in resettling immigrants from the former Soviet Union. Our nation has been built by their determination to be self-sufficient.
- *Patriotic:* Many immigrants want to learn English, and more would if classes were available.
- *Patriotic:* Many undocumented immigrants came here legally with visas for work, study, or travel. The visas expired and they became stranded when their money ran out. A good number would go home if they could afford to. Let's stop blaming and have a calm and rational conversation about immigration.

You can further flesh out your argument with denominational statements:

Central Conference of American Rabbis

The Central Conference "applauds and supports our nation's leaders who have called for comprehensive immigration reform, which would include not only better enforcement of our nation's laws, but also a guest worker program and a path to earned legalization."[1]

Unitarian Universalist Association

"All people—without regard to immigration status—deserve access to fair wages, education, housing, health care, and other social services; and immigrants are at high risk for being denied basic rights and services and thus warrant our special support."[2]

Presbyterian Church (USA)

"All people need an advocate and while Jesus is our advocate before God, Christians are called to advocate for the stranger—those in most need of justice."[3]

United Church of Christ

"[We] advocate for a policy that allows immigrant workers and their families to live and work in a safe, legal, orderly and humane manner through an Employment-Focused immigration program (as opposed to employer focused) that guarantees basic international workers' rights to organization, collective bargaining, job portability, religious freedom, easy and safe travel between the United States and their homeland, achievable and verifiable paths to residency, and a basic human right of mobility."[4]

The Rabbinical Assembly

The Rabbinical Assembly calls for "an immigration policy that allows the United States to attain its full economic potential; to create opportunities for earned legalization and a path to citizenship for undocumented immigrants already living in the United States."[5]

United Methodist Church

"As followers of Christ we are called to love the stranger in our midst because we were once strangers in a foreign land. The stranger in the midst at one time or another has been your own family member."[6]

Advocacy groups and government offices have up-to-the-minute information on immigration issues:

- American Immigration Lawyers Association (www.aila.org)
- Hebrew Immigrant Aid Society (www.hias.org)
- Interfaith Immigration Coalition (www.interfaithimmigration.org)
- National Immigration Forum (www.immigrationforum.org)
- U.S. Citizen and Immigration Services (www.uscis.gov)
- U.S. Committee for Refugees and Immigrants (www.refugees.org)

The Child Welfare Triangle

Opponents of policies protecting children and their families may well denounce government programs as bloated and inefficient. That message triangle might look like this:

Small government means cutting unessential programs for children, like education:
- Families need to care for themselves and not seek handouts from others.
- Kids need to be taught self-reliance, not to be dependent on society.
- We need to cut all the waste in school spending.

In this case, "Small government means cutting unessential programs for children, like education" becomes the following positive message: *Investing in children and their education builds our communities and America*.

"Families need to care for themselves and not seek handouts from others" becomes *Strong schools strengthen families*. "Kids need to be taught self-reliance, not to be dependent on society" becomes *Schools teach kids self-discipline and how to function properly in society*. And "We need to cut all the waste in school spending" becomes *Investing in the future ensures America will continue to be a world leader*.

Strong schools
strengthen families.

Investing
in children
builds America.

Schools teach kids
self-discipline.

Education makes
America a world leader.

Now let's put some talking points on the triangle:

Investing in children and their education builds our communities and America:
- *Pastoral:* As a pastor, I have seen quality child-care programs teach kids how to be social. These initiatives enable parents to go to work and provide for their families.
- *Community:* School breakfast and lunch programs are important to many families I know. The programs supplement strong education, wholesome family life, and the vitality of our community.
- *Patriotic:* As someone involved in the education of children, I believe sports, art, and music education teach kids to be productive members of society.
- *Pastoral:* I am a pastor and I think it's just common sense. Parents can become partners with schools and build our society when they have the necessary resources, including health care and housing.

Strong schools strengthen families:
- *Pastoral:* As a counselor to children and families, I see it every day. Parents can't do it all on their own, no matter their standard of living.
- *Pastoral:* I am mandated to report child abuse. I know how schools and other family support programs protect vulnerable kids from harm.
- *Community:* As we see in our Sunday school, supplemental programs make an essential contribution to children and families.

Schools teach kids self-discipline and how to function properly in society:
- *Pastoral:* My many years in religious education demonstrate that all kids are capable of learning social and academic skills.
- *Pastoral:* I help prepare young adults to lead an entire congregation in prayer at a Bar or Bat Mitzvah. I know the importance of good reading skills in growing to become a productive adult.
- *Pastoral:* As a counselor to teens and families, I can assure you that giving kids what they need helps them make wise decisions and one day become responsible family members.

- *Pastoral:* I teach in our religious education program. My experience demonstrates that classroom discipline is important to quality education.
- *Community:* Schools teach kids to provide for themselves and to work with others.
- *Personal:* Speaking as a parent, I don't want my kids to be deprived of a structured school experience that prepares them for the future.

Investing in the future ensures America will continue to be a world leader:

- *Patriotic:* In the long run, the cost to our nation of not addressing poverty—unemployment, hunger, loss of education, crime—is greater than the cost of addressing it.
- *Patriotic:* America can compete in the world marketplace when we make a meaningful investment in quality education.
- *Patriotic:* Investing in kids pays dividends for years to come, especially in this competitive world.
- *Patriotic:* All kids need to know reading and math. The nation's future depends on it.
- *Patriotic:* Ensuring our youngest members have proper medical and dental attention gets them off to a good start to a productive life and to become healthy builders of a strong America.

The denominations have great statements on child welfare:

American Baptist Churches USA

"The General Board of ABCUSA called upon 'the American Baptist Churches USA and its constituent partners to make the issue of Children in Poverty a priority of prayer, advocacy, ministry and stewardship. Let it occupy us in our sanctuaries, our fellowship halls, our communities, and especially the halls of power.'"[7]

Episcopal Church

The church "dialogue[s] with members of their state legislatures on behalf of responsible welfare reform which would aid poor people, rather than penalize them."[8]

Evangelical Lutheran Church in America

"[We] urge congregations to work toward a Christ-centered, positive environment for children in families, congregations, and communities, and pray for the well-being of all children, but in particular for the poorest and most at risk; declare our congregations as 'safe havens' for all children; develop creative programs to meet the needs of children in the congregation and community with special emphasis on those who are hungry, homeless, abused, lonely, and subject to violence; advocate in collaboration with advocacy offices of this church in support of public policy that advances the well-being of children and their families and in opposition to policies that harm them; and work collaboratively with other congregations, Lutheran social ministry organizations, and groups that strive to help children thrive."[9]

Jewish Reconstructionist Federation

"That one child or adult should lack sustenance would be *dayenu* (enough) to raise our voices. That millions go hungry and die of starvation is a situation that demands our pursuit of a just and large-scale united response across religious, social, and political lines. We join our hearts and hands with all of you to pursue the Divine call to do what is just—to work to end hunger everywhere."[10]

United Methodist Church

"[We] acknowledge the responsibility of both parents and government to provide for the well-being of children. Welfare should ensure that children benefit from the active and healthy participation of parents—whether custodial or not—in their lives. The barriers to participation by married parents in federal programs should be removed. There should be no family caps and no full-family sanctions. Children should benefit from successful state efforts to collect child support assistance from non-custodial parents through increasing the amount of collected child support that children receive."[11]

Advocacy groups with the latest information on child welfare include the following:

- Children's Defense Fund (www.childrensdefense.org)
- FamiliesUSA (www.familiesusa.org)
- National Partnership for Women and Families (www.nationalpartnership.org)
- Coalition on Human Needs (www.chn.org)
- Center on Budget and Policy Priorities (www.cbpp.org)
- Zero to Three Policy Center (www.zerotothree.org/public-policy)

Church-State Separation in the Media

Church-state separation raises some of the most contentious community issues; local disagreements over public holiday observance are among the most pitched. If an issue rises as the holiday approaches, it's best to try to wait until after the holiday before stepping in. You'll likely encounter a calmer, less emotional atmosphere later on and have a more productive conversation. Give some thought to group support when raising the topic; go in with others. Chapter 4, on church-state separation, provides useful information, including denominational statements. This section includes talking points organized by platform theme and can be tailored to fit the issue:

The experience of a pastor and the caring community:
- I can tell you the pain a child feels to be excluded from a holiday program because of faith.
- My experience says we need to take special care when it comes to our children and faith in the public forum.
- As a religious leader, I believe that religion is best taught in the home and in the religious community—not in the schools.

Disassociation: "Don't lump me with them":
- Those who want the Bible taught in public school science class don't speak for me. Please don't paint me with that brush.
- Many people wrongly assume that all religious groups see something wrong in same-gender marriage. I want to correct that mistaken assumption: a wide variety of faith communities recognize

the importance of providing the opportunity for civil marriage for lesbians and gays. Our state must not enshrine religious restrictions.

- Those pastors opposed to contraception have a right to their teaching; their church is entitled to believe and practice as it does. But, as a person of faith, I have a very different approach when it comes to making health care available to the wider community.

The perspective of a community leader:

- Contrary to what many people think, there is more than one approach to the role of religion in community life.
- Religion is private, policy is public. Let's not confuse the two.
- The community is best served when religious holidays are observed at home and in the church—not in the school.

The personal voice: "I speak as a parent, husband, son, pastor, and more":

- As a parent, I want our schools to welcome children of all faiths.
- As a member of the community, I take great pride in the diversity of religious groups we have here.

Advocacy history: "Voices of faith have spoken about this for years":

- Our denomination has always affirmed that we need to keep government out of religion and religion out of government.
- The United States has a proud history of interfaith cooperation.
- Ours is a spiritually diverse nation, with a variety of religious beliefs and practices.

The patriotic argument:

- The richness of our spiritual life is a hallmark of national pride and strength.
- Our nation has long honored the boundary of separation between church and state.

For current information on the separation of church and state, please visit the following:

- American Civil Liberties Union (www.ACLU.org)
- Americans United for Separation of Church and State (www.AU.org)
- People for the American Way (www.PFAW.org)

Staying on Point by Deflecting Unrelated Questions

It happens all the time. A reporter starts a conversation on one topic—say, a local zoning stir-up, a question about a public school holiday observance. He or she then turns to something else—say, the mayor's reelection campaign, and the mayor happens to be a member of your congregation. You don't want to go near this topic. Expect reporters to ask questions that make sense to them, but not to you. You don't have to respond to those questions, even if the reporter asks repeatedly. Stay on point and just about any reporter will take the hint and go back to the original issue.

Even friendly reporters will change topics. Reporters are often writing about more than one story at a time, so it's natural for them to jump around. It may seem abrupt, but that's the nature of the business. Nevertheless, we are not there to answer their questions; they are there to report what we have to say. There are many ways to say the things that are on your mind without going into the unexpected and the unprepared. When it looks like you are getting into uncomfortable territory, get back to your point by using "bridge language" that returns the discussion to your triangle. Good bridge language lightly touches on the unwanted question and demonstrates that you recognized what you were asked. Then it quickly goes back to your topic. Do this well and it won't look like you are hiding or avoiding. And you won't embarrass yourself or the reporter.

Never repeat the unexpected question. You are always at risk of being edited down to appear to say what you didn't want to say. Instead, use language like this to build a bridge and get back: "That's a really, really good question. But I am here today to talk about the other issue. The United States has a proud history of interfaith cooperation." Another line could be "I know you are interested in that topic, but I want to make sure that this one point is understood. The community is best served when religious holidays are observed at home and in the church, not in the school."

Other examples of bridge language include the following:

2/19/18

- Yes, many people are concerned about that. Let's return to the point I was making, because there is something we need to underscore. My experience says we need to take special care when it comes to our children and faith in the public forum.
- I am glad you asked, and we can come back to that question some other time. Today, I want to emphasize that many undocumented immigrants came here legally with visas for work, study, or travel. The visas expired and they became stranded when their money ran out. A good number would go home if they could afford to. Let's stop blaming and have a calm and rational conversation about immigration.
- I'm not familiar with that issue. Because of my work with congregants and community members concerned with family planning, I am very well acquainted with the need for being able to get contraception.
- No, that's not what I am here to discuss. I want to get back to the point I just made. My experience as a pastor demonstrates that when it comes to health care, it is best to let the woman make the decision.
- I understand what you are saying, but let's return to that other issue, since there is something really important that we have to stress. As someone who goes to church regularly, I want to underscore the message of your editorial on terrorism. We have to stop equating violence with faith.

Staying Calm by Deflating Emotional Questions

Sometimes contrary and attacking arguments threaten to throw you off. These arguments come from the most supportive reporters as from anyone else. That happens when you hear:

- According to some sources, you are totally wrong …
- Experts say the opposite …
- What do you say to the person who disagrees with you?
- You know that others say that's nonsense.
- Reverend So-and-so totally disputes what you just said.

This kind of argumentative question may well get you angry and prompt you to say something you will later regret. Build your bridge with "deflator" language that lowers the tension. Here are some examples:

- Some people feel that way. But I think my approach is better. I believe ...
- That's a common misperception. So let's set the record straight by realizing ...
- People say that all the time. But the truth of the matter is ...
- Folks have all kinds of strong opinions about this issue. Let me underscore mine.
- I know that, but I think we can all agree ...

My favorite pitfall is "Give me a straight yes-or-no answer." The old fake forced choice! Try these:

- The correct response is "C. None of the above."
- It's really very complicated. Do you have the time to explore this?
- Let's talk about the nuances in between the options.

You'll be glad when that one is over.

Closing the Interview

When you come to the end of the interview, go back to the beginning, whether it's an op-ed, letter to the editor, interview, sermon, or Sunday school lesson. *Drive home your point.* Use language like this:

- Before we finish, I want people to know that it is important to remember that ...
- To sum it all up, if I might ...
- The best thing to realize is ...
- Three things to keep in mind ...

You are ready for your media call, first thing tomorrow morning. You'll be great.

Multiplying Your Impact

We all hear how print media is in a state of decline and electronic media is on the rise. Electronic media provides many opportunities to grow the impact of a citation.

Include your citation or a link to it on your Facebook page, your personal website, and your organization's Facebook page, bulletin, and website. Have your friends and organization members link to you on their Internet sites. Send your citation to advocacy groups, your denominational offices, and publications. Ask them to link to it.

Good luck!

10

Religion and Lobbying

It was my first lobbying visit, a meeting in the state capitol with the governor's staff, no less. The topic was sex education, and while I had opinions about the issue, I had no idea what to say. These were my instructions: "You are, first and foremost, a pastor. Talk about your work with teens and their families. Describe how you counsel and support them. Talk about what they need to stay safe and healthy."

When we got to the meeting, this is what I said: "From my experience counseling teens and families, I can tell you that teens walk around with lots of misinformation. They need to know the truth. I hope this bill moves ahead so our teens get the accurate information they need to keep themselves safe and healthy." It was that simple.

Overcoming Reluctance to Lobbying

When it comes to lobbying—and not lobbying—you may be familiar with these excuses:

"Senators don't listen to people like me. All they care about are the special interests." Policy makers pay careful attention, especially on the state level. As for special interests, everyone is a "special interest." Everyone has the right to make their voice heard. Whatever your concern, use your influence.

"All my elected officials are in sync with me—why waste their time telling them what they already know?" Elected officials hear plenty of religious opposition to sex education and marriage equality, such that their support and involvement may slip from their active agenda. It's not hard to see why. Government offices are busy. The staff is typically overworked and, as in any office, is inclined to respond to those who complain the most. It is critical for policy makers to hear from their constituents, especially when policy makers do right. Each one of us needs to pick up the phone and bolster the officials who want to stand up for us. Call, write, or e-mail to thank a senator for taking a courageous stand—encourage them to keep up the fight. Legislators often do the right thing and love a word of appreciation! Your call may well prompt them to go down the hall and encourage a wavering colleague to join the cause.

"Lobbyists and lobbying have a bad reputation. I don't want anything to do with it." You might remember Ross Perot, a 1992 presidential third-party candidate. His stump speech—in a folksy, down-home delivery—went on about lobbyists in thousand-dollar suits, alligator shoes, and blown-dry hair, as examples (or symptoms) of the ways lobbyists pamper and enrich themselves at the expense of the people. But that's not the lobbying I do, and it is not what you do either.

It's very different when it comes to lobbying for immigrant rights or for access to reproductive health care. We aren't asking anything for ourselves, other than religious freedom. We are there for someone else—*as advocates*—lending stature and voice to others who are afraid or unable to come forward. Our lobbying contributes a critical measure of moral authority, arising from our religious titles and positions, to those who possess little political sway of their own. Now that I reminded you about Ross Perot, you can forget about him. Go lobby. Look your best. Wear something that identifies you as a member of the clergy or a person of faith. I have a *kipah*; ministers will wear a clergy collar. We lobby as religious advocates for people in need.

"There are laws against religious lobbying. We could lose our not-for-profit status." No, the tax code allows for limited lobbying by organizations, and many organizations do. Our denominations have offices in Washington, D.C., and in state capitols nationwide. We are allowed to get involved in ballot initiatives, just as religious groups did when Proposition 8 repealed marriage equality in California. Religious organizations can support nonpartisan voter registration drives, hold educational candidate forums that are open to all candidates, and provide transportation to the polls on Election Day; it's all permitted. The law specifically prohibits religious organizations—like any other not-for-profit such as a museum, college, library, or hospital—from endorsing or opposing candidates for office. We don't use the pulpit, the bulletin, or announcements to tell people *who* to vote for.

Now that we agree on the importance of lobbying and that it is appropriate, let's get to the specifics and the "how." It's best to work with an advocacy group or your denominational social justice office. Advocacy groups, in particular, have current information—issue background, where legislation stands, bill names and numbers—and they follow the opposition. They also know where your policy maker fits in—history of sponsoring legislation, past public statements, and voting records. The advocates may well organize specific advocacy days and welcome the contribution of a religious perspective. Or they may coordinate a visit in the local office, saving you the time and trouble of traveling to the state capitol or to Washington, D.C. Cooperating with a group on a visit will bring you into contact with other advocates who approach the issues from a secular perspective—that opens doors for you, too.

Lobbying Starts with a Phone Call

Most people don't communicate with their elected officials. When it comes to the local and state levels, many people don't know even who their elected officials are. Some don't care, some don't vote, and some aren't even registered to vote. Yet talking to policy makers is a very important part of living in a democracy. It doesn't take much effort to let them know what you think.

3/2/18

Try this right now. Think of an issue that's important to you. Look up your Congress member's telephone number by visiting www.house.gov. Pick up the phone and call him or her. You'll likely get through on the first try and reach a very polite person. In a few sentences, introduce yourself as a constituent, describe the issue, and explain why it is important to you. *Be sure to say you are a person of faith—regular attendee at church services, a member of a synagogue, or a member of the clergy—but try to avoid mentioning the name of the institution. Mentioning your faith makes your call stand out.* Ask for—or express thanks for—your representative's support. It's that easy.

I used to find lobbying intimidating. I wasn't versed in the issues or the ways to present myself. I had relationships with elected officials; we had conversations about common concerns, but it felt funny to actually ask for something. The reality is that elected officials expect us to be asking for things; they're used to it because that's their job—to be asked. It's all in a day's work. Lobbying is the patriotic thing to do, an honest American tradition. We are supposed to keep informed, and we are supposed to inform our leaders and to tell them how to represent us. It's their responsibility to know what we believe and what we want. As much as I want them to like me, they want me to like them. They will listen to my "ask" and respond politely. Even if it looks like legislators don't care what we think, they better find out; it's what they need to do to properly represent us and to get reelected. They need to know about religion and what it stands for, just as they need to learn about building and maintaining highways and bridges and disposing the trash. They have staff to help them with all this, but when it comes to religious nuances, legislators may need our help and should welcome the opportunity to sit down and listen.

Religious leaders contribute faith perspectives to the conversation, making clear the moral and religious issues at the center. When an issue looks secular—be it over the budget, national security, defense, or the environment—we contribute the perspective of faith. When opponents of abortion or contraception make arguments that don't sound religious, supportive religious arguments get to the faith at the core. Opponents may carry on about reining in Medicaid costs, for instance, and when they get to the details, sure enough, they are talking about cutting coverage for contraception. Hmmm ... sounds suspiciously religious to me. Clergy as lobbyists achieve things that no one else can do: laying bare the religion at the heart of the policy debate.

Be sure to keep local government in mind, something many people overlook. Many times, a state, county, or city government can give us what we cannot get in Washington, D.C. For example, some states recognize marriage equality, while the federal government has not. States provided funding for stem cell research long before the federal government got around to it. And states made access to emergency contraception more available to rape victims before the federal government came forward.

Preparing for Your Visit

In preparing for your visit, your team leader may place your legislator in one of several categories: strong supporter, soft supporter, fence sitter, soft opponent, strong opponent, or someone new to the office without a voting record.

Strong Supporter

A strong supporter is a champion for your issue, someone who speaks with the press, introduces legislation, and encourages others to sponsor a bill. When meeting with a strong supporter, describe how deeply you appreciate the strength your supporter lends to this issue. Ask for suggestions on how you can help. And ask what is ahead, just over the horizon. Some people wonder, "All my representatives already do what I want them to do. Why should I bother them?" The reality is that they need to hear from you. Your legislators need the reassurance, and they need to be encouraged to stay the course and enlist others in the cause. Each one of us—in government and in private life—can always do more to bring about change.

Soft Supporter

A soft supporter votes for a bill but never takes the lead. The soft supporter is a great friend, and your meeting gives an opportunity to ask for an added measure of visible support. Start by expressing appreciation for past votes. Describe the strong support for the issue in the district. And if a bill is under consideration, ask as appropriate:

- Will you help push it through the committee?
- Will you ask the Speaker to send it to the floor for a vote?
- Will you join us at a press conference?
- Will you sign on as a cosponsor?
- Will you talk it up among your wavering colleagues?

Your advocacy group will be helpful.

Fence Sitter or Newly Elected Official

With a fence sitter, or someone new to the office who does not yet have a voting record, there is work to do. Sometimes a fence sitter says one thing and does another; your presence can help make a difference. Again, emphasize the depth of support in the faith community and the community at large. Begin by either thanking him or her for a vote in the past or by expressing disappointment for a negative vote. Talk about your hopes for the future.

Be a "pastor": recognize how difficult it can be to take a stand on a controversial issue, but point out how many people in the district are with you. Try to get your policy maker to talk about the issue. It can't be easy getting caught in the middle between people who have strong feelings about a sensitive issue. Tell a pastoral story with impact that clinches the support.

Soft Opponent

You may not be able to win over a soft opponent, but you can point out how a district is mixed and recognize the challenge in that situation. Again, underscore the religious support. At the end of the meeting, you may have to agree to disagree, but make sure to leave the door open to future conversations.

Strong Opponent

Good luck with the strong opponent. You may not get anywhere; you may even get a brush-off instead of an appointment. If you do meet and things get hot, don't get angry and don't argue. Speak respectfully but with conviction. Stay on your message triangle. Don't make personal attacks, and listen carefully to any response. At the end of the meeting, express thanks for the legislator's time and hope that the conversation continues. You can say things like, "We disagree. But I am glad we had a chance to meet face to face." If it gets really bad, leave early. Meeting done.

Things to Keep in Mind

Don't be upset or take offense if upon arriving you are told that the official is tied up and instead a member of the staff will be taking your meeting. The staff has the boss's ear. The staff may have more time for you and may even be more effective in conveying your message. Besides, this person may turn out to be a great contact for you in the future if you or someone in your faith community ever has a need. Plus, you never know where this staffer will be working in a year or two. For all you know, his or her name may be on the door next time you are in for a visit—you might even be remembered from back when.

Unless you hear otherwise, allow thirty minutes for the meeting, although it could take longer if your legislator has the time and wants to chat. Prepare a group agenda, assign a group leader, and plan a timetable that includes introductions, presentation of the issues (no more than one or two), and a closing summary of the discussion. Be sure to include a word of thanks. Assign parts. Plan to meet your group outside the office a few minutes early so the meeting can begin on time. Make sure all the group members introduce themselves by name and title, as if the person you are meeting with doesn't remember who you are. Emphasize that you are there in a personal capacity—not speaking for any organization. If you are a constituent, then say so. Describe any other connections.

Know your media stills, memorize your message triangle, and have a few talking points. Make sure you are comfortable talking about church-state separation, especially when it comes to reproductive health or others' efforts to legislate their religious restrictions or practices. Try to keep the conversation on message, even if the policy maker or others in the group stray. Have fact sheets and issue background material to leave behind; your denomination or advocacy group can provide them. Be prepared to tell a brief pastoral story, no more than a minute long. Or, you can take a minute to explain why all your pastoral experience points to the need for a particular law or policy.

If you are asked a question and don't know the correct answer, don't make it up; say that you will find out and get back to the official with accurate information. You do not represent your house of worship; speak in your own name only. And when it comes to an opponent, be firm but don't get angry. Follow up with a letter of thanks, restate your key points, and perhaps extend an invitation to an event at your place of worship.

Writing a Letter to a Policy Maker

When writing a letter to a policy maker, follow these tips: Limit yourself to one page and one issue. Put your "ask" in the first sentence, mention the bill number, and send a news clip or other supporting info. Do not overstate your points. Be respectful. You can find the address on a website. Be sure to check your spelling, especially the name of the legislator. Remember, your own legislator wants to hear from you, few others do, but you can write committee members, legislative committee chairs, Speakers of houses, and majority and minority leaders. While you cannot vote for them, your letter may touch on their concern for the political party.

Your house of worship probably straddles more than one district. You can voice your concerns to anyone who represents the community you serve, although be clear that you are speaking in your own name. Don't copy some script letter from a website. Write in your own voice. E-mail will do, but a letter or call is better. All communication gets counted. When an issue is important, go ahead and write those in federal and state executive branches, departments that serve education, oversee health care, monitor insurance, or register vehicles, as appropriate. The heads of these departments—federal cabinet members and state department commissioners—determine policy. Flag your calendar; write your letters on your birthday or some other notable occasion so they get done. If you already communicate with your elected and appointed officials, promise yourself that you will double the amount. My guess is that you will not be taking on an onerous burden. You will be demonstrating your trust in our nation and carrying out a patriotic act. You will be contributing your share to the growing good of our communities. You will be bringing your faith to life.

Don't Be Intimidated!

This all may sound like a lot, perhaps too much. If you are intimidated and have not yet begun the lobbying process, start with a few small steps. Call a reporter or an editor at the local newspaper—the daily or, if you live in a big city, one of the weeklies. Or you can try a local radio or TV station. Ask for an appointment. Say you'd like to come by and get acquainted. If it's a newspaper, tell them that even though you read each issue of their paper, you have never been in a newsroom before and you'd like to see how a paper is made. Or say something similar if your call is to someone on-air. Mentioning your place in the religious community, especially as a member of the clergy, will open doors.

It's important to have a relationship with the media, especially with a local or regional paper as well as radio and TV. Religious leaders are community leaders, just like media people; your lives intersect in so many ways. You share common interests in the local economy, culture, health care, schools, and elsewhere. A newsroom or a broadcast studio is filled with interesting people. Ask their opinions about community issues and local events. Tell them what happens in your house of worship and comment on—perhaps compliment them on—a recent editorial or the way they covered an issue. Bring materials that describe your religious community—an introductory brochure and recent newsletter. You might find yourself breaking through a lifelong bias against religion. This is a great opportunity to teach about the faith.

Media people want to know about you and your work, your opinions about health care, education, the economy, not-for-profit organizations, and other topics. You can emphasize what your faith has to teach about controversial issues and church-state separation. The folks you are meeting respect your title and community position. You have access to their readership, people they never get to meet. You have a finger on the pulse of their stakeholders. And, most critically, media professionals want to make a good impression on you. They want you to like them. When you get back to the office, you can write a letter of thanks. Then start working on your media plan. Perhaps you or someone in your congregation is already sending out press releases. After press releases comes the friendly letter to the editor, expressing appreciation for an article you liked. You can follow up with an op-ed carrying a positive clergy perspective on a local issue or a spiritual reflection as a holiday approaches. Editors love quality writing, especially when they don't have to pay for it. Just as Martin Buber taught, it all starts with relationships.

After calling a reporter, try the mayor, a Congress member, or your state representative. Or you can call the school superintendent or the chief of police—anyone in government. Ask for an appointment. Go over and have a conversation. Again, talk about the community. Be familiar with what they support; many advocacy group websites allow you to check a voting record online. Bring an invitation to an event at your house of worship. Perhaps you are comfortable having them extend a greeting from the podium or the pulpit. Suggest they stay after a service and chat with members at a reception. It's all perfectly appropriate, as long as your policy maker is not running for office at that moment. Relationships with elected and appointed officials increase the standing of the congregation, lay leaders, and clergy in a way that raises no reasonable objection.

This is all about lifting the standing of your faith community—all faith communities—in the eyes of community leaders. Again, don't take offense when you get to the mayor's office and are asked to meet with a staffer instead. Office holders are busy and rely on their staff, but don't get angry; take advantage of the opportunity.

Finally, if you listen to talk radio, call in with a question or comment when you find a conversation is interesting. Or try something relatively safe, like discussing a problem with your old car on NPR's *Car Talk*. It's virtually anonymous, especially on a national show—as long as you only give your first name. Some shows even allow for extended banter with the host or guests—what a great way to increase your comfort level! Some stations have talk-back lines—you call in to record a message that is replayed on-air, the easiest thing to do. These are just a few ways to begin. All in all, advocacy (media work and lobbying) is like anything else. It begins with relationships. We build on those relationships to drive home the point and effect change.

Epilogue

More Than Tolerance

There's fondness for the old saying, "Live and let live," as if a tolerance—putting up with each other—is as high a goal as anyone could hope to achieve. But this "cold peace" of tolerance falls far short of a higher religious ideal—the call to recognize the Divine in daily life.

Martin Buber's *I-Thou* relationship illustrates the spirituality between people. *I-Thou* means God dwells in the open, honest, and caring exchanges among us. *I-Thou* is more than tolerance—it means, in the very least, respectful communication, even with those who look at things differently than you or I do. In the spirit of Buber's teachings, I'd like to close this book by reflecting on a heroic story of interfaith cooperation and sacrifice during a crisis in U.S. history.

On February 3, 1943, the United States troop transport Dorchester carried more than nine hundred soldiers and crew across the North Atlantic Ocean to the battlefields of WWII. Just after midnight, a torpedo blast from a patrolling German submarine pierced the Dorchester's hull, immediately damaged the engine, tipped the ship to the side, and killed and injured many asleep in multiple-level bunks below deck. The captain, recognizing that the ship was doomed, began an evacuation protocol that included caring for the wounded, tossing sensitive files overboard to keep them from enemy hands, and sending surviving crew and soldiers into life boats.

However, it became quickly obvious that vital life boats and life preservers were damaged or lost in the torpedo blast, and that many would soon die in the cold water. Now the story turns to the heroism of the ship's four chaplains—Methodist minister The Rev. George L. Fox, Rabbi Alexander D. Goode, Roman Catholic priest The Rev. John. P. Washington, and Reformed Church in America minister The Rev. Clark V. Poling—for a profound lesson on the power and impact of faith.

"Just before the ship went down," said Daniel O'Keefe, a nineteen-year-old survivor of the tragedy, "the chaplains gave their life preservers to members of the crew. They were standing on the deck praying when our lifeboat drifted out of sight."[1] Other witnesses reported that the chaplains offered their gloves and life vests to soldiers without even asking their faith, linked arms in chanted prayer—Latin, Hebrew, and English—and went down with the ship.[2]

Four chaplains of four denominations stood arm-in-arm under one flag of the United States of America as the ship descended into the dark, cold waters of the North Atlantic that mid-winter night. It was a bold, clear, brave, patriotic, and exemplary affirmation of bonds of faith across religious lines.

Life rarely calls a person to such heroism and sacrifice. And each one of us is left to wonder what we would do in a situation like that one. But this example speaks to the potential for noble action and the call to the faithful to act in a way that blesses the lives of others.

At first, it might seem that this act of religious heroism has little to do with questions of social policy and faith. Yet, their story has a lesson for us. One organization established to honor the chaplain's memory asks, "If they can die together, why can't we live together?"[3] They looked beyond religious differences with a nobility that calls us to do the same. And we can begin to follow their example with honest and respectful conversation, the kind of conversation that begins with respectful listening.

I took my first lessons on listening as a congregational rabbi and pastor to people in hospitals, nursing homes, and other residential settings. I'd typically walk into a room like a nurse, dietician, doctor, or any other person on the staff and jump right into a conversation about whatever topic the person wanted to discuss—a serious medical decision, urgent family need, or something routine. For the most part, they'd talk and I'd try to pay careful attention.

I'd often walk into a room to find a TV tuned to a program that sparked a conversation. When I served synagogues in New England and stormy weather was expected, folks watched the Weather Channel and our chat turned to the bad weather. When I worked in the Boston area during the 2004 baseball World Series, it seemed everyone hoped the Red Sox would clinch their first pennant in eighty-six years. During election season, you guessed it, political talk shows brought our conversations to personalities and issues. Folks, even when infirm or ill, care about politics—and they vote.

As you might imagine, I had to be careful with political conversations. After all, I was a pastor and a guest in those rooms. When I heard sharp or harsh opinions, I had to remind myself that I was not a campaign worker, that it was my place to listen nonjudgmentally. When I was asked for an opinion, I'd give it, and when our perspectives differed, I respectfully and caringly spoke my mind under the umbrella of agreeing to disagree. I'd often ask clarifying questions, all the while mindful that, as a pastor, I was there to listen, reflect, support, and show that I care—not to achieve a political end. These experiences showed me how clergy share in the lives of others, and I took the lessons into my advocacy work with a goal of achieving dialogue founded on careful and respectful listening. Respectful listening leads to respectful conversation and, I pray, eventually and hopefully opens to love.

We all have a lot to learn from the example of the four chaplains. Their lesson is one we would do well to master now. The spiritual and moral destiny of our nation and communities are at stake over how we communicate our religious differences; respectful conversation contributes to the betterment of our country and world. So let us begin, today, with words. 3/2/18

Amen

Notes

Chapter 1. Why We Hear So Much from One Side and So Little from the Other

1. This data comes from the article "With Synagogues in Jeopardy, It's Time to Talk about Tithing," by Dennis S. Ross and Robert Evans, *The Jewish Daily Forward*, April 24, 2008.

2. Representative Boehner's comments are from the press release, "Speaker Boehner on the Ryan Budget: If the President Won't Lend, We Will," April 15, 2011, www.speaker.gov/News/DocumentSingle.aspx?DocumentID=237235 (accessed November 12, 2011).

3. President George W. Bush, as quoted in "Bush Remarks Roil Debate on Teaching of Evolution," by Elisabeth Bumiller, *New York Times*, August 3, 2005.

Chapter 2. Core Faith Values: Protecting the Widow, the Stranger, and the Orphan

1. "Clerics Urge Jerusalem to Ban Gay Pride," by Amriam Barkat and Daphna Berman, March 31, 2005, www.haaretz.com; and "Clerics Fighting a Gay Festival for Jerusalem," by Laurie Goodstein and Greg Myre, *The New York Times*, March 31, 2005.

2. Pastor John Hagee's comments as quoted in "Will MSNBC Devote as Much Coverage to McCain's Embrace of Hagee's support as It Did to Obama's Rejection of Farrakhan?" February 28, 2008, www.MediaMatters.org; and "Hagee Says Hurricane Katrina Struck New Orleans Because It Was 'Planning a Sinful' Homosexual Rally,'" by Matt Corley, April 23, 2008, www.ThinkProgress.org.

3. Yusuf Abu Sneina's comments from "Tyrant USA Will Fall," in Palestinian Media Watch, September 9, 2006, www.palwatch.org/main.aspx?fi=623&doc_id=784 (accessed December 24, 2011).

4. Ovadiah Yosef's comments from "Shas Rabbi: Hurricane Is Bush's Punishment for Pullout Support," September 7, 2005, www.Haaretz.com, Associated Press.

5. William Ryan, *Blaming the Victim*, rev. ed. (New York: Vintage Books, 1976).

6. The Cheyenne and Seattle instances were cited in "The Chinese Must Leave: Cheyenne Workingmen Give Warning to the Celestials," *New York Times*, September 29, 1885; "The Chinese in Augusta," *New York Times*, October 28, 1885; and "Labor in California: The Chinese Must Be Driven Out, but Not Enough Men Left," *New York Times*, November 29, 1885.

7. All translations of the Hebrew Bible and Rabbinic literature are by the author.

8. George Wallace, as quoted in "Hecklers Disrupt Talks by Wallace," by Walter Rugaber, *New York Times*, October 2, 1968.

9. Talmud, Berachot 10a.

10. Midrash, Genesis Rabbah 12:15.

Chapter 3. Core Faith Values: Moral Agency

1. See Rev. Tom Davis, *Sacred Work: Planned Parenthood and Its Clergy Alliances* (New Brunswick, N.J.: Rutgers University Press, 2005), for a detailed history of clergy advocacy for reproductive rights, including the Clergy Consultation Service on Abortion.

2. From "Facts on Induced Abortion in the United States," Guttmacher Institute, August 2011, www.guttmacher.org/pubs/fb_induced_abortion.pdf (accessed November 12, 2011).

3. "Report of the South Dakota Task Force to Study Abortion: Submitted to the Governor and Legislature of South Dakota," December, 2005, p. 67.

4. Ibid., p. 56.

5. "The Baptist Faith and Message," www.sbc.net/bfm/bfm2000.asp#xviii (accessed November 12, 2011).

6. Mike Huckabee, as quoted in "Between Pulpit and Podium, Huckabee Straddles a Fine Line," by David D. Kirpatrick and Michael Powell, *New York Times*, January 19, 2008.

7. "American Baptist Resolution Concerning Abortion and Ministry in the Local Church," www.abc-usa.org/LinkClick.aspx?fileticket=HJ4sJT1lqzg%3D&tabid=199 (accessed November 12, 2011).

8. "The Truth about Catholics and Abortion," Catholics for Choice, 2011, www.catholicsforchoice.org/documents/TruthaboutCatholicsandAbortion.pdf (accessed January 18, 2012).

9. "Reform Judaism: A Centenary Perspective," Central Conference of American Rabbis, 1976, http://ccarnet.org/rabbis-speak/platforms/reform-judaism-centenary-perspective/ (accessed January 18, 2012).

10. "No. 0725 (Sense-of-the-Assembly) Proactive Prevention: Seeking Common Ground on the Issue of Abortion," www.disciples.org/Portals/0/PDF/ga/pastassemblies/2007/resolutions/0725.pdf (accessed November 12, 2011).

11. "Reaffirm General Convention Statement on Childbirth and Abortion," Archives of the Episcopal Church, www.episcopalarchives.org/cgi-bin/acts/acts_resolution-complete.pl?resolution=1994-A054 (accessed November 12, 2011).

12. "We Affirm: Religions Support Reproductive Choice," Religious Coalition for Reproductive Choice, http://rcrc.org/pdf/we_affirm_2010.pdf (accessed November 12, 2011).

13. "Reproductive Rights," Union for Reform Judaism, http://urj.org//about/union/governance/reso//?syspage=article&item_id=1904 (accessed November 12, 2011).

14. "Right to Choose," Unitarian Universalist Association of Congregations, www.uua.org/statements/statements/14499.shtml (accessed November 12, 2011).

15. "Abortion," United Methodist Church, www.umc.org/site/apps/nlnet/content.aspx?c=lwL4KnN1LtH&b=5066287&ct=6467539 (accessed November 12, 2011).

Chapter 4. Core Faith Values: Church-State Separation

1. From "2010 Legislative Wrap Up," Center for Reproductive Rights, p. 14, http://reproductiverights.org/sites/crr.civicactions.net/files/documents/state_wrapup_2010.pdf (accessed January 18, 2012).

2. "Nuns Back Bill amid Broad Rift over Whether It Limits Abortion Enough," by Helene Cooper, *New York Times*, March 19, 2010.

3. Bart Stupak, as quoted in "BlogTalk: Progressives, Public Opinion and Abortion," in The Caucus, *New York Times*, March 19, 2010.

4. "Address of Senator John F. Kennedy to the Greater Houston Ministerial Association," September 12, 1960, www.jfklibrary.org/Research/Ready-Reference/JFK-Speeches/Address-of-Senator-John-F-Kennedy-to-the-Greater-Houston-Ministerial-Association.aspx (accessed November 12, 2011).

5. *Church and State*, May 2009; *New York Times*, November 16, 2009.

6. "Thomas Jefferson's Letter to the Danbury Baptists," Americans United for Separation of Church and State, January 1, 1802, http://au.org/files/images/page_photos/jeffersons-letter-to-the.pdf (accessed December 24, 2011).

7. "Forbidding Everything Like an Establishment," in *What God Has Put Asunder: James Madison Quotes on Church and State*, Americans United for Separation of Church and State, http://au.org/files/images/page_photos/what-god-has-put-asunder.pdf (accessed December 24, 2011).

8. "American Baptist Resolution on Separation of Church and State," www.abc-usa.org/LinkClick.aspx?fileticket=Pm1kkXvrrqM%3d&tabid=199 (accessed November 12, 2011).

9. "Policies and Procedures," Evangelical Lutheran Church in America, www.elca.org/What-We-Believe/Social-Issues/Policies-and-Procedures.aspx (accessed November 12, 2011).

10. "Separation of Church and State," Union for Reform Judaism, http://urj.org//about/union/governance/reso//?syspage=article&item_id=2254 (accessed November 12, 2011).

11. "Separation of Church and State," Unitarian Universalist Association of Congregations, www.uua.org/statements/statements/13424.shtml (accessed November 12, 2011).

12. "Separation of Church and State," United Methodist Church, http://archives.umc.org/interior_print.asp?ptid=4&mid=6742 (accessed November 12, 2011).

13. "Separation of Church and State in the United States (1997)," United Synagogue of Conservative Judaism, http://uscj.org/Aboutus/Resolutions/ResolutionsbyYear/_1997/SeparationofChurchandStateintheUnitedStates.aspx (accessed November 12, 2011).

Chapter 5. Messaging to the Base

1. John Kyl's remarks as quoted in *Think Progress,* April 8, 2011.

2. All quotations that follow from Gov. George Wallace are from his 1963 Inaugural speech, Alabama Department of Archives and History, 1963.

3. George Wallace, as quoted in "By Trial and Error, Wallace Shapes His Platform," by Ben A. Franklin, *New York Times,* September 1, 1968.

4. "Wallace, in City, Says U.S. Suffers," by Linda Charlton, *New York Times*, December 5, 1970.

5. "George Wallace, Symbol of the Fight to Maintain Segregation, Dies at 79," by Howell Raines, *New York Times*, September 15, 1998.

6. Ronald Reagan, as quoted in "'Welfare Queen' Becomes Issue in Reagan Campaign," *New York Times,* February 15, 1976.

Chapter 8. Building and Using a Message Triangle

1. Ronald Reagan, as quoted in "Washington Talk; The Presidency: Reagan and His 'Golden Oldies,'" by Steven V. Roberts, *New York Times*, July 16, 1987.

Chapter 9. Building on the Triangle: The Platform of Faith

1. "Immigration Reform," Central Conference on American Rabbis, http://data.ccarnet.org/cgi-bin/resodisp.pl?file=immigration&year=2006 (accessed November 12, 2011).

2. "Unitarian Universalist Association Policy on Immigration," Unitarian Universalist Association of Congregations, www.uua.org/immigration/57099.shtml (accessed November 12, 2011).

3. "Advocacy: Putting Love of Neighbor into Action," Presbyterian Church, http://oga.pcusa.org/immigration/pdf/advocacy.pdf (accessed November 12, 2011).

4. "A Call for More Humane U.S. Immigration Policy; End Migrant Deaths; Support Immigrant Communities," United Church of Christ, www.ucc.org/synod/resolutions/immigration-final.pdf (accessed November 12, 2011).

5. "Resolution on Immigration to the United States," Rabbinical Assembly, www.rabbinicalassembly.org/resolution-immigration-united-states (accessed November 12, 2011).

6. "Call for Comprehensive Immigration Reform," United Methodist Church, www.umc.org/site/apps/nlnet/content2.aspx?c=lwL4KnN1Lt H&b=4951419&ct=6480715&notoc=1 (accessed November 12, 2011).

7. "American Baptist Home Mission Societies Children in Poverty Initiative," American Baptist Church, www.abcopad.org/Docs/ Children%20in%20Poverty%20Grant%20Proposal%202011a.pdf (accessed November 12, 2011).

8. "Request Dioceses to Address the Effects of Welfare Reform," Archives of the Episcopal Church, www.episcopalarchives.org/ cgi-bin/acts/acts_resolution.pl?resolution=1997-A050 (accessed November 12, 2011).

9. "Safe Haven for Children," Evangelical Lutheran Church in America, www.elca.org/What-We-Believe/Social-Issues/ Resolutions/1999/CA99,-p-,03,-p-,03-Safe-Haven-for-Children.aspx (accessed November 12, 2011).

10. "Resolution on Mazon, a Jewish Response to Hunger," Jewish Reconstructionist Federation, http://jrf.org/node/1034 (accessed November 12, 2011).

11. "Principles of Welfare Reform," United Methodist Church, http:// archives.umc.org/interior_print.asp?ptid=4&mid=921 (accessed November 12, 2011).

Epilogue

1. "Former Rabbi Listed as Missing at Sea, One of Four Chaplain Heroes of Sinking," *New York Times*, March 27, 1943.

2. "Summary of Statements by Survivors SS DORCHESTER, Passenger-Cargo Vessel, 5654 G. T., Merchants-Miner Transportation Co., Operated by AGWI Lines, Inc., Chartered to Army Transport Service," www.armed-guard.com/dork.html (accessed January 13, 2012).

3. Immortal Chaplains Foundation, http://immortalchaplains.org/ home.htm (accessed January 27, 2012).

Suggestions for Further Reading

Cohen-Keiner, Andrea. *Claiming Earth as Common Ground: The Ecological Crisis through the Lens of Faith.* Woodstock, VT: SkyLight Paths Publishing, 2009.

Davis, Rev. Tom. *Sacred Work: Planned Parenthood and Its Clergy Alliances.* Piscataway, New Jersey: Rutgers University Press, 2005.

Friedman, Maurice. *Martin Buber: The Life of Dialogue.* London: Routledge, 2002.

Goldberg, Michelle. *Kingdom Coming: The Rise of Christian Nationalism.* New York: W. W. Norton, 2007.

———. *The Means of Reproduction: Sex, Power, and the Future of the World.* New York: Penguin, 2009.

Hacala, Sara. *Saving Civility: 52 Ways to Tame Rude, Crude & Attitude for a Polite Planet.* Woodstock, VT: SkyLight Paths Publishing, 2011.

Internal Revenue Service. "Tax Guide for Churches and Religious Organizations." Washington, D.C.: Department of the Treasury Internal Revenue Service, 2009.

Lakoff, George. *Don't Think of an Elephant: How Democrats and Progressives Can Win.* White River Junction, VT: Chelsea Green, 2005.

Luntz, Frank. *Words That Work: It's Not What You Say, It's What People Hear.* New York: Hyperion, 2006.

Mackenzie, Don, Ted Falcon, and Jamal Rahman. *Getting to the Heart of Interfaith: The Eye-Opening, Hope-Filled Friendship of a Pastor, a Rabbi & an Imam.* Woodstock, VT: SkyLight Paths Publishing, 2009.

———. *Religion Gone Astray: What We Found at the Heart of Interfaith.* Woodstock, VT: SkyLight Paths Publishing, 2011.

Ross, Dennis S. *God in Our Relationships: Spirituality between People from the Teachings of Martin Buber.* Woodstock, VT: Jewish Lights Publishing, 2003.

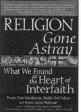
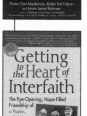
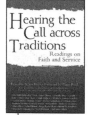

Spiritual Practice

Fly Fishing—The Sacred Art: Casting a Fly as a Spiritual Practice
by Rabbi Eric Eisenkramer and Rev. Michael Attas, MD
Illuminates what fly fishing can teach you about reflection, awe and wonder; the benefits of solitude; the blessing of community and the search for the Divine.
5½ x 8½, 192 pp (est), Quality PB, 978-1-59473-299-7 **$16.99**

Lectio Divina—The Sacred Art: Transforming Words & Images into Heart-Centered Prayer *by Christine Valters Paintner, PhD*
Expands the practice of sacred reading beyond scriptural texts and makes it accessible in contemporary life. 5½ x 8½, 240 pp, Quality PB, 978-1-59473-300-0 **$16.99**

Recovery—The Sacred Art: The Twelve Steps as Spiritual Practice
by Rami Shapiro; Foreword by Joan Borysenko, PhD
A hope-filled approach to spiritual and personal growth, using the Twelve Steps of Alcoholics Anonymous uniquely interpreted to speak to everyone seeking a freer and more God-centered life.
5½ x 8½, 240 pp, Quality PB, 978-1-59473-259-1 **$16.99**

Haiku—The Sacred Art: A Spiritual Practice in Three Lines
by Margaret D. McGee 5½ x 8½, 192 pp, Quality PB, 978-1-59473-269-0 **$16.99**

Dance—The Sacred Art: The Joy of Movement as a Spiritual Practice
by Cynthia Winton-Henry 5½ x 8½, 224 pp, Quality PB, 978-1-59473-268-3 **$16.99**

Spiritual Adventures in the Snow: Skiing & Snowboarding as Renewal for Your Soul
by Dr. Marcia McFee and Rev. Karen Foster; Foreword by Paul Arthur
5½ x 8½, 208 pp, Quality PB, 978-1-59473-270-6 **$16.99**

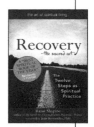

Divining the Body: Reclaim the Holiness of Your Physical Self *by Jan Phillips*
8 x 8, 256 pp, Quality PB, 978-1-59473-080-1 **$16.99**

Everyday Herbs in Spiritual Life: A Guide to Many Practices
by Michael J. Caduto; Foreword by Rosemary Gladstar
7 x 9, 208 pp, 20+ b/w illus., Quality PB, 978-1-59473-174-7 **$16.99**

Giving—The Sacred Art: Creating a Lifestyle of Generosity
by Lauren Tyler Wright 5½ x 8½, 208 pp, Quality PB, 978-1-59473-224-9 **$16.99**

Hospitality—The Sacred Art: Discovering the Hidden Spiritual Power of Invitation and Welcome *by Rev. Nanette Sawyer; Foreword by Rev. Dirk Ficca*
5½ x 8½, 208 pp, Quality PB, 978-1-59473-228-7 **$16.99**

Labyrinths from the Outside In: Walking to Spiritual Insight—A Beginner's Guide
by Donna Schaper and Carole Ann Camp
6 x 9, 208 pp, b/w illus. and photos, Quality PB, 978-1-893361-18-8 **$16.95**

Practicing the Sacred Art of Listening: A Guide to Enrich Your Relationships and Kindle Your Spiritual Life *by Kay Lindahl 8 x 8, 176 pp, Quality PB, 978-1-893361-85-0* **$16.95**

Running—The Sacred Art: Preparing to Practice *by Dr. Warren A. Kay; Foreword by Kristin Armstrong 5½ x 8½, 160 pp, Quality PB, 978-1-59473-227-0* **$16.99**

The Sacred Art of Chant: Preparing to Practice
by Ana Hernández 5½ x 8½, 192 pp, Quality PB, 978-1-59473-036-8 **$15.99**

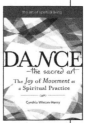

The Sacred Art of Fasting: Preparing to Practice
by Thomas Ryan, CSP 5½ x 8½, 192 pp, Quality PB, 978-1-59473-078-8 **$15.99**

The Sacred Art of Forgiveness: Forgiving Ourselves and Others through God's Grace
by Marcia Ford 8 x 8, 176 pp, Quality PB, 978-1-59473-175-4 **$18.99**

The Sacred Art of Listening: Forty Reflections for Cultivating a Spiritual Practice
by Kay Lindahl; Illus. by Amy Schnapper 8 x 8, 160 pp, b/w illus., Quality PB, 978-1-893361-44-7 **$16.99**

The Sacred Art of Lovingkindness: Preparing to Practice
by Rabbi Rami Shapiro; Foreword by Marcia Ford 5½ x 8¼, 176 pp, Quality PB, 978-1-59473-151-8 **$16.99**

Sacred Attention: A Spiritual Practice for Finding God in the Moment
by Margaret D. McGee 6 x 9, 144 pp, Quality PB, 978-1-59473-291-1 **$16.99**

Soul Fire: Accessing Your Creativity
by Thomas Ryan, CSP 6 x 9, 160 pp, Quality PB, 978-1-59473-243-0 **$16.99**

Thanking & Blessing—The Sacred Art: Spiritual Vitality through Gratefulness
by Jay Marshall, PhD; Foreword by Philip Gulley 5½ x 8½, 176 pp, Quality PB, 978-1-59473-231-7 **$16.99**

Women's Interest

Women, Spirituality and Transformative Leadership
Where Grace Meets Power
Edited by Kathe Schaaf, Kay Lindahl, Kathleen S. Hurty, PhD, and Reverend Guo Cheen

A dynamic conversation on the power of women's spiritual leadership and its emerging patterns of transformation.
6 x 9, 288 pp, Hardcover, 978-1-59473-313-0 **$24.99**

Spiritually Healthy Divorce: Navigating Disruption with Insight & Hope
by Carolyne Call A spiritual map to help you move through the twists and turns of divorce. 6 x 9, 224 pp, Quality PB, 978-1-59473-288-1 **$16.99**

New Feminist Christianity: Many Voices, Many Views
Edited by Mary E. Hunt and Diann L. Neu

Insights from ministers and theologians, activists and leaders, artists and liturgists who are shaping the future. Taken together, their voices offer a starting point for building new models of religious life and worship.
6 x 9, 384 pp, HC, 978-1-59473-285-0 **$24.99**

New Jewish Feminism: Probing the Past, Forging the Future
Edited by Rabbi Elyse Goldstein; Foreword by Anita Diamant

Looks at the growth and accomplishments of Jewish feminism and what they mean for Jewish women today and tomorrow. Features the voices of women from every area of Jewish life, addressing the important issues that concern Jewish women.
6 x 9, 480 pp, Quality PB, 978-1-58023-448-1 **$19.99**; HC, 978-1-58023-359-0 **$24.99***

Bread, Body, Spirit: Finding the Sacred in Food
Edited and with Introductions by Alice Peck 6 x 9, 224 pp, Quality PB, 978-1-59473-242-3 **$19.99**

Dance—The Sacred Art: The Joy of Movement as a Spiritual Practice
by Cynthia Winton-Henry 5½ x 8½, 224 pp, Quality PB, 978-1-59473-268-3 **$16.99**

Daughters of the Desert: Stories of Remarkable Women from Christian, Jewish and Muslim Traditions
by Claire Rudolf Murphy, Meghan Nuttall Sayres, Mary Cronk Farrell, Sarah Conover and Betsy Wharton
5½ x 8½, 192 pp, Illus., Quality PB, 978-1-59473-106-8 **$14.99** Inc. reader's discussion guide

The Divine Feminine in Biblical Wisdom Literature
Selections Annotated & Explained
Translation & Annotation by Rabbi Rami Shapiro; Foreword by Rev. Cynthia Bourgeault, PhD
5½ x 8½, 240 pp, Quality PB, 978-1-59473-109-9 **$16.99**

Divining the Body: Reclaim the Holiness of Your Physical Self
by Jan Phillips 8 x 8, 256 pp, Quality PB, 978-1-59473-080-1 **$16.99**

Honoring Motherhood: Prayers, Ceremonies & Blessings
Edited and with Introductions by Lynn L. Caruso 5 x 7¼, 272 pp, HC, 978-1-59473-239-3 **$19.99**

Next to Godliness: Finding the Sacred in Housekeeping
Edited by Alice Peck 6 x 9, 224 pp, Quality PB, 978-1-59473-214-0 **$19.99**

ReVisions: Seeing Torah through a Feminist Lens
by Rabbi Elyse Goldstein 5½ x 8½, 224 pp, Quality PB, 978-1-58023-117-6 **$16.95***

The Triumph of Eve & Other Subversive Bible Tales
by Matt Biers-Ariel 5½ x 8½, 192 pp, Quality PB, 978-1-59473-176-1 **$14.99**

White Fire: A Portrait of Women Spiritual Leaders in America
by Malka Drucker; Photos by Gay Block 7 x 10, 320 pp, b/w photos, HC, 978-1-893361-64-5 **$24.95**

Woman Spirit Awakening in Nature: Growing Into the Fullness of Who You Are
by Nancy Barrett Chickerneo, PhD; Foreword by Eileen Fisher
8 x 8, 224 pp, b/w illus., Quality PB, 978-1-59473-250-8 **$16.99**

Women of Color Pray: Voices of Strength, Faith, Healing, Hope and Courage
Edited and with Introductions by Christal M. Jackson
5 x 7¼, 208 pp, Quality PB, 978-1-59473-077-1 **$15.99**

The Women's Torah Commentary: New Insights from Women Rabbis on the 54 Weekly Torah Portions
Edited by Rabbi Elyse Goldstein
6 x 9, 496 pp, Quality PB, 978-1-58023-370-5 **$19.99**; HC, 978-1-58023-076-6 **$34.95***

* A book from Jewish Lights, SkyLight Paths' sister imprint

Religious Etiquette / Reference

How to Be a Perfect Stranger, 5th Edition: The Essential Religious Etiquette Handbook *Edited by Stuart M. Matlins and Arthur J. Magida*

The indispensable guidebook to help the well-meaning guest when visiting other people's religious ceremonies. A straightforward guide to the rituals and celebrations of the major religions and denominations in the United States and Canada from the perspective of an interested guest of any other faith, based on information obtained from authorities of each religion. Belongs in every living room, library and office. Covers:

African American Methodist Churches • Assemblies of God • Bahá'í Faith • Baptist • Buddhist • Christian Church (Disciples of Christ) • Christian Science (Church of Christ, Scientist) • Churches of Christ • Episcopalian and Anglican • Hindu • Islam • Jehovah's Witnesses • Jewish • Lutheran • Mennonite/Amish • Methodist • Mormon (Church of Jesus Christ of Latter-day Saints) • Native American/First Nations • Orthodox Churches • Pentecostal Church of God • Presbyterian • Quaker (Religious Society of Friends) • Reformed Church in America/Canada • Roman Catholic • Seventh-day Adventist • Sikh • Unitarian Universalist • United Church of Canada • United Church of Christ

"The things Miss Manners forgot to tell us about religion."

—*Los Angeles Times*

"Finally, for those inclined to undertake their own spiritual journeys ... tells visitors what to expect." —*New York Times*

6 x 9, 432 pp, Quality PB, 978-1-59473-294-2 **$19.99**

The Perfect Stranger's Guide to Funerals and Grieving Practices: A Guide to Etiquette in Other People's Religious Ceremonies *Edited by Stuart M. Matlins*
6 x 9, 240 pp, Quality PB, 978-1-893361-20-1 **$16.95**

The Perfect Stranger's Guide to Wedding Ceremonies: A Guide to Etiquette in Other People's Religious Ceremonies *Edited by Stuart M. Matlins*
6 x 9, 208 pp, Quality PB, 978-1-893361-19-5 **$16.95**

Inspiration

Saving Civility: 52 Ways to Tame Rude, Crude & Attitude for a Polite Planet
by Sara Hacala
Offers a definitive look at what civility means and how it can change the nature of everyday interaction.
6 x 9, 240 pp, Quality PB, 978-1-59473-314-7 **$16.99**

Restoring Life's Missing Pieces
The Spiritual Power of Remembering & Reuniting with People, Places, Things & Self
by Caren Goldman
A powerful and thought-provoking look at reunions of all kinds as roads to remembering and re-membering ourselves.
6 x 9, 208 pp, Quality PB, 978-1-59473-295-9 **$16.99**

How Did I Get to Be 70 When I'm 35 Inside?
Spiritual Surprises of Later Life
by Linda Douty
Encourages you to focus on the inner changes of aging to help you greet your later years as the grand adventure they can be.
6 x 9, 208 pp, Quality PB, 978-1-59473-297-3 **$16.99**

Who Is My God? 2nd Edition
An Innovative Guide to Finding Your Spiritual Identity
by the Editors at SkyLight Paths
6 x 9, 160 pp, Quality PB, 978-1-59473-014-6 **$15.99**

God the What?
What Our Metaphors for God Reveal about Our Beliefs in God
by Carolyn Jane Bohler
6 x 9, 192 pp, Quality PB, 978-1-59473-251-5 **$16.99**

About SKYLIGHT PATHS Publishing

SkyLight Paths Publishing is creating a place where people of different spiritual traditions come together for challenge and inspiration, a place where we can help each other understand the mystery that lies at the heart of our existence.

Through spirituality, our religious beliefs are increasingly becoming a part of our lives—rather than *apart* from our lives. While many of us may be more interested than ever in spiritual growth, we may be less firmly planted in traditional religion. Yet, we do want to deepen our relationship to the sacred, to learn from our own as well as from other faith traditions, and to practice in new ways.

SkyLight Paths sees both believers and seekers as a community that increasingly transcends traditional boundaries of religion and denomination—people wanting to learn from each other, *walking together, finding the way.*

For your information and convenience, at the back of this book we have provided a list of other SkyLight Paths books you might find interesting and useful. They cover the following subjects:

Buddhism / Zen	Global Spiritual	Monasticism
Catholicism	Perspectives	Mysticism
Children's Books	Gnosticism	Poetry
Christianity	Hinduism /	Prayer
Comparative	Vedanta	Religious Etiquette
Religion	Inspiration	Retirement
Current Events	Islam / Sufism	Spiritual Biography
Earth-Based	Judaism	Spiritual Direction
Spirituality	Kabbalah	Spirituality
Enneagram	Meditation	Women's Interest
	Midrash Fiction	Worship

Or phone, fax, mail or e-mail to: SKYLIGHT PATHS Publishing
Sunset Farm Offices, Route 4 • P.O. Box 237 • Woodstock, Vermont 05091
Tel: (802) 457-4000 • Fax: (802) 457-4004 • www.skylightpaths.com
Credit card orders: (800) 962-4544 (8:30AM–5:30PM EST Monday–Friday)
Generous discounts on quantity orders. SATISFACTION GUARANTEED. Prices subject to change.